AROUND THE HELFORD

Round Walks from Gillan to Falmouth

Front cover
Gillan (or Carne) Creek, Walk 2, December 1994
(photograph by Katherine Farmer)

Back cover
Top: Mawgan Cross, Walk 7
Bottom: Porthnavas Creek at Trenarth Bridge, Walk 10

Drawing on page 1
Manaccan as seen near the end of Walk 1

Drawing on opposite page
Polwheveral Creek, Walk 9

Not "Scissor Man", but the intrepid author, armed with map and watched by admiring granddaughter, crossing the slippery stepping stones near the mouth of Gillan or Carne Creek - part of the South West Way, and a possible link between Walks 1 and 2. See pages 12 and 17.   (Photograph by Katherine Farmer)

Landfall Walks Books No.4

BOB ACTON

AROUND THE HELFORD

Round Walks from Gillan to Falmouth

First published 1989
Reprinted with slight revisions, 1990
Third edition, fully revised, 1995

LANDFALL PUBLICATIONS

Landfall, Penpol, Devoran, Truro, Cornwall TR3 6NW
Telephone: Truro (01872) 862581

MY THANKS TO .....

all the people who have so willingly and even enthusiastically helped with
information about local history, particularly the Vicars of Constantine, St
Mawgan and Manaccan and the owners of Roskruge Barton, Trenarth
Manor, Kiln House at Bishop's Quay and The Sanctuary at Mawnan. Since
publishing the first edition I have received very helpful information from,
among others, Mrs Vanessa Beeman, Mr Raymond Nicholls and especially
Mr Alan Bean, who has gone to great trouble to explain the complexities of
the paths around Trecoose, as well as himself doing an excellent job in
helping to maintain those paths. I am also grateful to the authors of the
books which have proved most useful: see the list on page 87. Last and
most, of course, my thanks to Viv in her capacity of wife and mentor, as
well as the co-author of two of the said books.

Typesetting and illustrations by Bob Acton

Printed by the Troutbeck Press
and bound by R. Booth Ltd., Antron Hill, Mabe, Penryn, Cornwall

CONTENTS

Key Map

There is a larger sketch map for each walk or group of walks, but I recommend you to use the relevant Ordnance Survey maps in addition when out on the walks. These are "Landranger" Nos. 203 & 204; and, best of all for walkers, "Pathfinder" maps, "Helford River", "Falmouth & St Mawes" and "Helston & Prussia Cove".

"Sunday Afternoon Specials": See page 86.

INTRODUCTION

This is a companion volume to *Around the Fal*; like that one, it presents a series of round walks chosen both for the natural beauty of the areas through which they pass and also for the historical interest of various features along the way. As with the Fal, much of the shoreline on the upper reaches of the Helford is privately owned and inaccessible to walkers; a pity, perhaps, but on the other hand "developers" too have been kept out - and there are still many fine walks beside the river and its creeks, along the nearby coast and through the peaceful, unspoilt country a little way inland, as I hope the book will prove.

As always, I have tried hard to make the directions clear and accurate, and to ensure that all routes are on public rights of way or permissive paths, but there are bound to be some lapses on my part, and also various changes on and around the routes may create unexpected problems. I am always pleased to hear about such things. Once a gentleman rang me to complain that there were two bulls in a field I had directed him to cross in *A View from Carn Marth*; there was no sign of them a few days later when we went to check. Some other sorts of snag do require looking into, though, and I have passed several readers' letters on to the Highways Department in the hope of prompting some action on their part; failing that, at least the letters have alerted me to changes that may need making to future editions of the books.

I've received a few complaints that the walks in my books are too long. If you agree, page 86 is for you.

Bob Acton - October 1989

NOTE TO THE THIRD EDITION

After more than five years, it has been necessary to do a thorough revision. The inclusion of a sketch map for each walk or group of walks, along with considerably expanded notes on points of interest, plus a complete extra walk, will, I hope, persuade some readers who already have the original book to invest in the new one! I have walked most of the routes again, revising directions where necessary. I concentrated mainly on the sections where I knew there were likely to be problems; the very wet spell of weather we had early in 1995 foiled my original plan to cover every walk in full, so there are probably still some errors lurking unsuspected in the following pages. If you discover them, please let me know - and I hope they won't spoil your enjoyment.

Bob Acton - February 1995

USING THIS BOOK

Before you set off, please read the introductory remarks for the walk in question, which will give you some hints about such things as the sort of footwear needed, how tough or easy the walk is, and whether you will be able to find refreshments en route. In some cases, too, you could increase the pleasure of the walk by making prior arrangements, such as telephoning for permission to visit certain sites. The opening dates and times of certain houses, gardens, etc., are generally included in the italicised notes.

Directions are given in **bold type**, and the symbol (*) refers you to an *italicised note*. In the directions, the paragraph numbers such as ❶, ❷, ❸, etc., correspond to the numbered points on the sketch map for that walk.

A few very short circular walks, based on the longer routes, are suggested. These are indicated on the maps by the symbol ✿.

The book has a waterproof cover and will fit easily when open into the sort of clear polythene bag used in supermarkets to wrap fruit and vegetables ..... so there's no need for rainy weather to prevent you from doing the walks. The sketch maps are not drawn very precisely to scale, and give only a rough idea of the route, but you should be in no danger of going astray if you follow carefully the very detailed directions. Even so, if you can take along the relevant Ordnance Survey Landranger or Pathfinder map your understanding of what you see will be further enhanced, and you will have the opportunity to explore this splendid region for yourself. Details about the OS maps covering the area are given at the top of the Key Map on page 5.

WALK 1
MANACCAN, ROSKRUGE, FLUSHING & GILLAN
A little under five miles. For a much shorter round walk, see page 86.

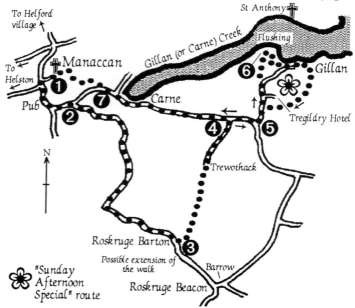

Gillan Creek has often been described as the Helford in miniature. It's certainly a place of great charm and beauty, and the area around Flushing and Gillan Coves benefits from being inaccessible to motorists, apart from the few who are fortunate enough to live there. The first part of this walk is through lush, rolling countryside, a mixture of woods and farmland, passing interesting and historic old farms, and with occasional views of Gillan (or Carne) Creek, the Helford and the coast beyond. Most of the route is along minor roads, normally little-used except by farm vehicles; about one mile is on a slightly busier but still usually quiet road. About half a mile is on footpaths across fields, and here you may need waterproof footwear; about a mile is on well-made tracks; and nearly half a mile follows the coastal footpath - a well-used section which is unlikely to be muddy. There are a few quite steep hills. Manaccan, where the walk starts and ends, is one of my favourites among inland Cornish villages, with lots of beautiful old cottages clustered cosily around its ancient church. It has a thriving, well stocked general store and a popular pub, the New Inn, whose appearance belies its name. The Tregildry Hotel at Gillan serves bar food.

8

To drive to Manaccan (*) from Helston, take the A3083 Lizard road, turning left on to the B3293 road to St Keverne at the roundabout just beyond RNAS Culdrose (HMS Seahawk). After about two miles turn left to Newtown-in-St Martin; there turn right and almost immediately left, following signs to Manaccan and Helford. Finally turn right along a narrow road through Tregonwell to Manaccan. At the T-junction in the village you may find room for parking immediately ahead; if not, turn left and then right, where there is a space near the church and the village shop. From Falmouth, take the B3291 from Penryn to Gweek; after the second bridge at Gweek take the left turning, joining the B3293 near Garras; from there continue via Newtown-in-St Martin as already described.

MANACCAN

Pronounced "M'nac'n", the village's name seems to derive from the church's dedication to "Sancta Manaca". Nothing whatever is known about any such saint; the church at Lanreath is dedicated to St Manakneu, who could be the same person. Another possibility is that the word means "place of monks"; there is no evidence of a monastery ever having been here, but an alternative old name for the parish was "Ministre", and it is in the region called Meneage, "the monkish land".

Quite a lot of the 12th century Norman church remains; the tower was built in the 14th and 15th centuries, when the church was enlarged. What the very informative booklet available in the church calls a "drastic restoration" took place at the end of the 19th century: the roof, for example, was replaced, but some of its carved timber was used to make the pulpit and chairs in the chancel. Further additions and alterations have been made more recently. Outside, there is of course the famous old fig tree, still growing strong after some two centuries, and apparently finding nourishment in the stone wall; in fact, the wall is filled with rubble at the centre, and the tree has rooted in the earth below that. Something similar has happened at St Newlyn East church. Notice, too, the chain attached to the south wall of the tower; the village stocks were once secured by it.

Easily the most famous of Manaccan's many incumbents was Richard Polwhele (vicar, 1794-1822), the poet and local historian. The story is told in some local books that on one occasion he threw Captain Bligh of the Bounty into the village lock-up (later used as the vicarage coal-cellar) while he finished his meal; but Polwhele's own account of the incident - included in A.S.Oates' book - is quite different. At the time, Bligh was carrying out survey work, and this led some parish constables to suspect that he was a French spy. The vicar, who was also the local magistrate and head of the recently-formed militia, was not at home, so it was decided to lock the stranger in a room recently added to the vicarage, to await Polwhele's return. Not surprisingly, Bligh was furious, but the incident ended amicably, with the vicar and the captain chatting till the small hours.

❶ Walk down the road, passing the well (restored in honour of the Queen's Silver Jubilee, 1977) and the New Inn, **down quite a steep hill to Tregonwell Mill and over the bridge. Follow the road round to the left, signposted to St Anthony, Flushing, Porthallow and Gillan.**

❷ After a few hundred yards, take the narrow, uphill road on the right: quite a strenuous climb, but the countryside is lovely, and when you reach the first attractive old farm (Lannarth or Lanarth, whose name probably means "clearing in the woods") there are fine views, first of Gillan Creek and then of the coast. The pretty house on the left later is Boden Vean (pronounced Bo<u>den</u>, and probably simply meaning "small dwelling"). Now the road passes through woodland as it approaches the historic Roskruge Barton (*).

ROSKRUGE

The name of this beautiful old house means "the barrow on the moor", referring to the burial mound at the nearby Beacon. Parts of the late medieval house remain, but it was largely rebuilt in late Tudor times by a family of minor gentry who took their name from the house, and was probably enlarged late in the 17th century. A list of the contents dated 1605 shows a busy, self-sufficient household, and one fully prepared for self-defence: muskets, pistols, cullivers, bows and corselets are included. The present owners told me that a crossbow and corselet (body armour) were found in the small room on pillars above the main entrance. In the outbuildings were larder, fish-house, dairy and rooms for spinning and weaving; there is also a cellar, which seems likely to have been used originally as a byre: the warmth from the cattle would have helped heat the parlour above. In later years the cellar was probably used for making and storing cider. A stone from a cider press can be seen on the left as you walk between the house and the outbuildings. As was the fashion at the time, a parlour was built in a wing, and it had a high plaster barrel ceiling. V.M. and F.J.Chesher, from whose book, "The Cornishman's House" I have taken most of these details, point out the kitchen's "huge external stack which dominates the gable like a tower". The owners believe that the footpath passing Roskruge was originally a Pilgrims' Way linking St Anthony church, where there was once a monastery, with another monastery at Trewothack and a Saxon chapel of St James of Compostella at Tregowris, which is south of Roskruge. A.S.Oates mentions an escape route passing Roskruge for people who had sought sanctuary at St Keverne church; this was along the road via Manaccan to the ferry at Treath, near Helford.

❸ Immediately beyond the house, turn left, following the Public Footpath sign, on to the drive that runs between the house and its outbuildings, the first of which was a mill; it has been altered very little since it was built in the early or mid 19th century.

Roskruge

NOTE: *Before taking this turning, you might care to walk a further half-mile-or-so along the road to Roskruge Beacon. At 378 feet above sea level, this is claimed by Charles Henderson to be the highest point on the Lizard peninsula; the same claim is made about "The Mount" in the Trelowarren Woodland Walk leaflet. If you turn left at the T-junction and then cross the stile on your left nearly opposite the turning to Tregarne, you will find a barrow - ancient burial-mound - and a view which has few rivals on any walk in this book. The barrow looks well preserved, but in fact, as Canon Trevor McCabe, Vicar of Manaccan, pointed out in the parish magazine, it "has, well within living memory, been ploughed down and then restored by order of the Ancient Monuments Commission!" From there, return to Roskruge Barton.*

Go through the five-bar wooden gate beside the cottage, again following a Public Footpath sign, walk to the left along the field edge for about fifty yards, and then veer to the right, cutting off the field corner, to a footbridge and stile beside a third footpath sign. You will probably encounter mud here. Step up to the field on the right and follow the left edge of it. Ignore the gates near the corner; continue round the corner and cross the rather high stile over the wall on your left. Now go straight across the field ahead, aiming just to the right of the cottage at

Trewothack ("stream farm" - but I didn't see a stream), **and cross the stile in the wall there, easily missed because not much of it remains. Turn left - in other words, keep walking in roughly the same direction - and go straight along the farm drive,** which before long gives you a superb view across Falmouth Bay. **After a modern bungalow the drive becomes a public road which runs down to the "main" road at Gillywartha** ("the higher grove").

④ At the T-junction turn right; from here there is a view of the Helford.

⑤ After a few hundred yards, just before the Gillan Garage, take the left turning with a sign advertising the Tregildry Hotel. Not far beyond the hotel entrance, the road bends quite sharply to the right, and there is a sign ahead, The Round. Here go straight on along the side road. The many modern bungalows here may remind you momentarily of suburbia, but that thought will soon be dispelled by the view over the creek on the right and then later of St Anthony Church on the left.

⑥ When you reach the coastal footpath at the bottom, you could first go a few yards to the left, down to the foreshore close to the stepping stones which at low tide provide a short if somewhat treacherous cut to the church; but **to continue the walk, turn right.** Soon you reach the **attractive sandy beach at Flushing Cove (*). Continue along the coast path to Gillan Cove (*), and here it's worth crossing the footbridge to the old quay at Gillan Harbour and the small headland beyond, called The Herra** (or perhaps more correctly "The Erra", meaning "the field").

St Anthony Church from Flushing Cove

FLUSHING AND GILLAN

Flushing takes its name from Vlissingen in Holland, possibly because Dutch workmen were employed to build sea walls, as at Flushing in Mylor parish, but more probably because Dutch ships and their crews were frequent visitors to harbours like this. As at Helford Passage, "trigging" - digging for cockles on the foreshore - is a Good Friday custom at Flushing.

"Gillan" simply means "creek"; according to Jill Newton, Gillan Creek should be called "Durra" (= "water"), from the name of the stream that enters it at Carne. I have also been told by an old inhabitant of the area that the proper name is Carne Creek, so on the sketch maps I'm playing safe. The harbour at Gillan seems to have been quite a busy port in the Middle Ages: documents from that time mention the shipping of leather, salt, fish and fish products. From the 16th century there are records of tin shipments; Jill Newton suggests that the tin must have come from some small mines at Goonhilly.

Return across the bridge and turn left at the foot of the slope, beside the gate to Gillan Cove House, on to the pretty lane which curves up through the wooded valley. Continue past Tregasso (the name appears to mean "dirty farm", but if so I'm sure the reason has vanished long ago!). **At the road, turn left, and then at the T-junction turn right to return to Manaccan. The walk now keeps to this road for about a mile;** please take care, because the traffic, though rarely if ever heavy, can be fast. Just beyond Carne ("rock"), the road hugs the edge of Gillan (or Carne) Creek for a few yards at Mennava, formerly Carne Mill. The older part of the large white house on the opposite side of the creek was also once a watermill, Penpol Mill; for some information about that, see the note at the end of Walk 2.

❼ Ignore the right turning signposted to St Anthony, but soon afterwards turn right at the Public Footpath sign, over a footbridge and up into the woods. Notice the well-preserved but dry leat (artificial watercourse), which once fed Penpol Mill: it is up on your right at first, and then the footpath crosses it. **After climbing quite steeply, with several stiles along the way, the path emerges into an open field. Follow the hedge on your left, crossing two more stiles, and at the lane turn left. This soon returns you to Manaccan church.**

WALK 2

MANACCAN, BOSAHAN, DENNIS HEAD & ST ANTHONY

About four and a half miles. Extension to Helford would add nearly a mile. For a very short walk around Dennis head, see page 86.

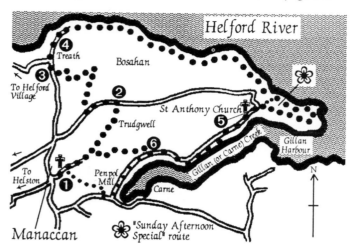

Manaccan certainly deserves a second visit, and this walk based on it is particularly fine. Except for the first mile-or-so and a short final section, it's all by water, first the Helford and then Gillan (or Carne) Creek. The latter is a wonderful place for birdwatching, especially at low water: among the myriad more common water-birds we saw there the last time we did this walk - just before Christmas 1994 - were several snow-white egrets .... or was it just the one bird, keeping us company as we went?   En route are two beautiful old churches (Manaccan and St Anthony), a headland giving spectacular views, and the Bosahan estate, where you may be able to visit the deservedly famous 5-acre valley garden if you choose your day carefully. (Details of opening days and times are given in the "Gardens of Cornwall Open Guide", published annually by the Cornwall Garden Society.) A short diversion would enable you to include Helford village on the walk. The second half of the route is mainly along a minor road - one which carries quite a lot of summer traffic - but a creekside footpath runs just below the road for much of its length. Mud is not likely to be a severe problem anywhere on this walk, but please don't take that as a firm

14

promise! The going is quite easy, for the most part, but there are some steep ups-and-downs on the later part of the Helford River section, and the path along here can be both slippery and rather overgrown. Refreshments - both shops and pubs - are available at Manaccan and Helford. There are at least three pleasant bathing beaches which you could use.

PLEASE NOTE: The coastal footpath passing through the Bosahan estate is permissive, not a public right of way, and the owners have placed a ban on dogs, so if you want to walk from Manaccan to St Anthony with your dog(s) I'm afraid you'll have to use the road, turning right at the T-junction (point 2) and picking up the directions again at point 5.

Directions for driving to Manaccan and parking there are given for Walk 1.

① Start by walking up the church steps, past the famous fig-tree, through the gate ahead and up the lane beyond that, following a Public Footpath sign. Where the main track bears slightly right, signposted to St Anthony, fork left over a stile. You cross a second stile before reaching the aptly-named Trudgwell Farm, where a sign on a cage warns of man-eating guinea hens. Ignore the footpath sign to the right: continue up the surfaced road.

② At the T-junction, turn left, towards the Goonhilly dishes, passing the entrance to Bosahan. About a hundred yards after that, cross the granite cattle-grid on your right, following the footpath sign. After a second grid and two kissing-gates, turn left on a surfaced lane. At the end of the first field on the right, go through the second gate on the right, signposted to Helford. Keep by the hedge on the right for about 40 yards, then go left across the field to a stile beside a footpath (to St Anthony) sign.

③ Turn right on the road.

Now EITHER, to visit Helford, follow the footpath sign on the left; at the first field-boundary go right through the kissing-gate; walk down to the road and keep straight on for Helford. To continue the walk, take the coast path from the car park, picking up the directions again at point 4.

OR, to keep to the shorter route, ignore the footpath sign and continue down the road as far as the sharp left corner at Treath. (For some information about Treath, see the end of the note on Helford, Walk 3.) Bear right on to the concessionary footpath which runs for a mile or more through the wooded margins of the Bosahan (*) estate.

BOSAHAN

The name, meaning "house in the dry place", is pronounced "B'zayn". The gardens were planted late last century by Sir A.P.Vivian, who had collected many exotic plants on his travels in Australia and the tropics. The impressive Tudor-style house which he built, and which served as a training centre for the Women's Land Army in World War II, was replaced by a more modest mansion in 1956.

❹ Watch for coast path signs; most of the left turns are side-paths going down to the foreshore. The village opposite at first is Helford Passage, and later comes Durgan. You pass - and may if you wish go down to - three small coves with beaches; from each a pleasant (but private) valley path leads inland towards the house, and you may well see or at least hear some of Bosahan's ornamental pheasants. **Beyond the third cove comes quite a steep climb; soon you emerge from the wood into a shrubby area, and finally after a kissing-gate into open fields. Keep to the left side of the fields, crossing two stiles and passing navigation aids in the form of two poles, one red-and-white and the other bearing a red triangle.** After this you can glimpse St Anthony church tower on the right. **Continue on the left over another stile and up rough steps to a kissing-gate. Now you could cut across to the church on the right, but it's far better to go on to Dennis Head (*).**

DENNIS HEAD

The name means "fort", and the trenches and banks across the neck of the promontory are probably at least two thousand years old, but in 1643 new defences were built by the Royalists under the command of Sir Richard Vyvyan of Trelowarren (see Walk 6), and the work done then is hard to distinguish from the original fortifications. Sir Richard endured financial ruin, having personally borne most or all of the costs of maintaining the garrison. Dennis Fort surrendered to Fairfax in March 1646, five months before the fall of Pendennis Castle at Falmouth, but for some years after that it retained a garrison of Parliamentary soldiers. For details of Dennis Fort, see Mary Coate, pages 121-4.

For Dennis Head, cross the wooden stile soon on the left (notice, near that, the remains of the old ramparts), **and then you can circle the headland in a clockwise direction**, getting superb views, first of the coast as far as Dodman Point and even, in clear conditions, to Rame Head near Plymouth; and then, as you round the corner, of Gillan Creek. **Return to the wooden stile, go a few yards to the right and then bear left towards the creek, through a kissing-gate and down to the church at St Anthony.**

ST ANTHONY-IN-MENEAGE

The church rivals St Just-in-Roseland and Mylor for the beauty of its waterside setting. The word "Meneage" (pronounced "M'neeg" or "M'nayg"), in use for this area at least as long ago as 967, means "monkish land"; some historians have obligingly detected several likely monastic sites in the region, though the evidence for many of them looks rather slender. The Rev. H.H.Dixon's view, given in the excellent little church booklet, is that there was probably a monastery here, as suggested by the name of the church farm, Lantinning (Lan-Intenyn, monastery of St Intenyn); Oliver Padel, however, explains "lan" as "church-site", so some doubt remains.

The granite in the church tower is of a type found in Normandy but not Cornwall, so there may be a germ of truth in the legend that the church was founded as a thank-offering to their saint by shipwrecked Normans. St Anthony was Egyptian; since his emblem was a pig, local people rejoice in the nickname of "St Anthony pigs" and their parish feast (26 December) is called Piggy Feast. From the Conquest to the Reformation, the parish belonged to the priory of Tywardreath, near Fowey, which is the focus of the historical parts of Daphne du Maurier's "The House on the Strand".

Parts of the church, including much of the chancel, date back to the 12th century, but it was greatly enlarged in the 15th; the carved oak wagon roof is from that time. I am told this church is probably the only one in Cornwall still depending on candlelight. Outside, notice the sealed-up "dog door" or "cat flap" in the west door of the tower; Dixon suggests it may in fact have been cut to allow hens to roost in the belfry! (Liz Luck in "South Cornish Harbours" quotes an anonymous diary dated 1885 describing the "appalling state" of the church: "Were it intended to house a litter of pigs it could hardly be considered a tidy sty.") Nearby, next to a very worn and battered old Celtic cross, there is a chain to which the stocks were attached, as at Manaccan church.

❺ At the road turn right.

(At low tide you could walk along the foreshore for the first few hundred yards, but then the deep-water channel runs too close to this side for further progress. In any case, the going on the foreshore is mostly too rough for comfort.)

Walking along the road, you will soon see a path leading down on the left; if you want to get across to the Gillan side of the creek you can do so at low water by taking this path and then walking a short way up-river to where there are some rather rough and slippery stepping-stones.

But for this walk, **continue along the creekside road until you see another path down to the left with a National Trust sign forbidding the digging of bait for commercial purposes.** Although the road is perfectly acceptable and indeed delightful for walking on, the footpath closer to the creekside is even better. Some care is needed, though, because it can be rather slippery; and unless it has been recently cleared it may be overgrown with brambles in places. **Soon after you have passed a group of tall Monterey pines, the path returns you to the road, which itself then descends almost to water-level.**

❻ Very soon after that, a stream passes under the road, and the road curves left and starts to rise again. Here, turn sharp right on to the footpath signposted to Manaccan (*but see the italicised note below for a recommended variation of this part of the route*) - a pretty path by a tiny stream - possibly muddy in places. **Soon you pass among the attractive buildings of Roscaddon,** one of which dates from 1597; **and a little way beyond that the path re-joins the track along which you walked at the start.**

NOTE: If you still have time and strength to spare, I would recommend you first to continue a little further along the road to look at what was once Penpol Mill. You will recognise it easily by the millstones laid out on both side of the road beside it. Notice, too, the course of the leat (millstream) under the road, and the remains of the waterwheel occupying part of the space between the older building and the modern extension. From the mill you could either return to the path just mentioned, or continue to the T-junction, turn right, and then cross the footbridge to join the path signposted to Manaccan, as described at the end of Walk 1.

St Anthony-in-Meneage

WALK 3
HELFORD VILLAGE, MUDGEON &
FRENCHMAN'S CREEK

About five miles. See page 86 for shorter version omitting Mudgeon.

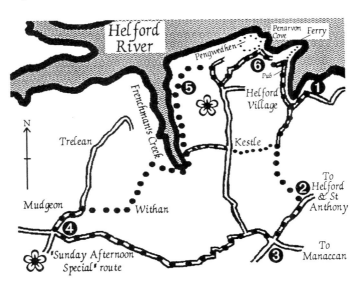

Here is some of the loveliest scenery in all Cornwall..... If I'm exaggerating, put it down to the fact that I'm writing this immediately on returning home; the walk that's freshest in my mind usually seems the best. This one starts and ends at an impossibly pretty village; next comes a wooded valley; then a couple of miles on minor roads with fine views of rolling farmland and other wooded valleys; a path through fields brings you to what must surely be among the most famous, yet still one of the least known, of all creeks; next comes a track on high land with good views towards the mouth of the Helford; and finally one more wooded valley leading to a small cove and a short circular woodland walk (optional) before you reach the Shipwright's Arms at Helford - or, if you prefer, cream teas at Rose Cottage, or some rather special ice-creams at the Post Office and general store. The route is fairly hilly and includes a long climb near the end of the road section. Please note: in winter or after rainy spells at any time, the path is likely to be very muddy on both sides of Withan Farm, between Mudgeon (I'll firmly resist the temptation to pun) and Frenchman's Creek; the same applies to the point where you cross the stream in that creek; if you don't have

19

wellingtons or something similar, I suggest that you limit yourself to the shorter walk described on page 64.

Drivers coming from Helston or Falmouth should follow the directions given for Walk 1, but go straight on instead of taking the right turn through Tregonwell. Helford has a large, well-signposted car park with toilets.

❶ The Mission Church of St Paul, beside the car park entrance, was built at the end of the 19th Century as a "chapel of ease" to save villagers the long walk to Manaccan. In the turret once hung a bell taken from the square-rigged ship Bay of Panama after she was wrecked off the coast nearby during the Great Blizzard of March 1891. Since 1982, however, the building has ceased to be a church (it's now a craft shop), and the bell has been in Manaccan belfry. **To start the walk, leave the car park by the path beside the church and go down the road into Helford (*). When you reach the footbridge, don't cross it** (unless you want to use the shop or pub) **but take the footpath signposted to Manaccan, passing several thatched cottages.** Soon you are walking up a beautiful wooded valley, with the stream on your right. The first side-path crossing the stream leads to Kestle farm and Frenchman's Creek: this is the shorter route given on page 64. **For the full walk, continue ahead up the valley. Eventually the path crosses a stone footbridge and starts to climb more steeply.**

HELFORD

Although protected from the worst ravages of the motor car, Helford has paid a price for its picturesqueness: Sarah Foot, in "Rivers of Cornwall", writes of "Emmie Hewett, the last Cornishwoman to live in Helford. Even she will be gone soon to live in Manaccan." Houses in Helford now are too expensive for most "locals", and in winter the village is almost deserted. "Yet," says Miss Foot, "there is still a community feeling here, though many of the inmates are relative newcomers."

It must have been very different when the fishing-boats were operated by men from the village rather than St Keverne, Cadgwith or even further afield; and even more so in 1724 when Daniel Defoe wrote about "Helford .... where many times the tin-ships go in to load for London". Another account, from 1814, described a quay big enough to take boats of 300 tons, plus a large storage cellar. There are many tales of smuggling involving the village, and the Shipwright's Arms is said to have extra-thick walls to accommodate contraband goods. A.S.Oates in "Around Helston in the Old Days" (1951) writes, "As late as 1840 the Custom House at Helford was besieged by about 30 men who broke locks, smashed doors, and carried off 126 kegs of contraband brandy which had been seized by the revenue officials from a cargo brought from Roscoff..."

The ferry operates from Helford Point now, west of the inlet, but for many centuries the landing place was at Treath, to the east, whose name actually means "ferry"; Bronze Age remains found at Treath suggest that the crossing here may be very ancient indeed.

Several stories about the use of the Shipwright's Arms by men involved in the secret operations during World War II are told in "Operation Cornwall" and "Cornish War and Peace".

❷ **Immediately after crossing the first stile beyond the bridge, turn right through a small metal gate and walk up beside the hedge on the right. At the top, a stile brings you to the road. Turn right.** Please be careful, as this road can be busy in summer. Soon you pass Myrtle Cottage, with its fuchsia hedges, and the large Manaccan Methodist Church on a high spot with panoramic views.

❸ **Take the first right turn, signposted to Kestle and Mudgeon; ignore the next turning (to Kestle Wartha), and either continue along the road or cross the stile on the left and walk across the field to the right, soon reaching another stile back to the road. This cuts off a corner, but the stiles tend to be rather overgrown.** The road passes the attractive house and outbuildings of Tregithew farm, and descends to a pretty valley down which flows one of the streams that empty into Frenchman's Creek. The view to the right from the gate just beyond is one of my favourites in this area. Now the road goes steeply down to the main valley leading to the creek; at the lowest point there was once a ford, and the old footbridge remains. Next there is quite a long haul uphill, past Carnbarges ("buzzard tor": the owners rang me some time ago to say that six breeding buzzards were still there) and the entrance to Withan ("tree") Farm. At the top is Mudgeon Cot.

MUDGEON

This fine old house is unfortunately not visible from the public road, but you might be able to get the owners' permission to look at it. In some ways it resembles Roskruge (Walk 1), since it's of similar age (early 17th century) and also has a parlour wing. Its staircase is said to be especially fine. Mudgeon manor itself is much older: it is mentioned in a legal document of 1324. When John St Erth built the new house, "New House" is what he called it, but using the Cornish language, "Chynoweth", and then the family adopted that as their surname. The historian Hals states that about a century later the Chynoweth family inheritance was "all spent through luxury and ill-conduct" when the three heiresses married unwisely.

❹ Turn right at the crossroads, signposted to Mudgeon and Treveador. Keep right at the entrance to Mudgeon farm (*). Soon the road bends quite sharply left; about twenty yards beyond the corner, cross the concrete-block stile on the right.

(The road, by the way, continues down to Trelean, where a valley garden running down to the Helford has been created in recent years. An interesting "nature diary" about Trelean by the owner, G.T.Witherwick, has been published under the title, *In a Cornish Valley*. In *"Fangs"* Mr Witherwick gives his autobiography, culminating with the creation of the garden. The latter book is available at some local shops and direct from Landfall Publications.)

Cross the field to another stile, and continue in the same line towards Withan Farm. The next stile may be overgrown, and the gate beside it is hard to open but quite easy to climb. Now head for the field corner close to the farm; a stile (easier to get under than over) is just to the right of the round drinking-trough. Between here and the house is a patch that seems to be permanently boggy (you were warned!). After negotiating that, bear left, go through the metal gate and straight on to a second one. (This is another area which can be very mucky in wet weather; if you find it almost impassable, ask at the house. The owners tell me they can show walkers an easier way through.) Footpath signs now direct you round the left side of the field and through another metal gate. Keep beside the hedge on your right. (You are quite near Frenchman's Creek now, but it's very well hidden - hence, perhaps, its reputation as a secretive, even spooky place.) After the gap in the hedge ahead, turn right and make for the lowest part of the dip. Now the path enters the wood and follows the valley-bottom down to the creek. The path turns right, and may be a little overgrown. After a few yards you can walk down to the stream (watch out for boggy patches), and there are several points where fallen trees or stepping-stones make it easy to cross. Getting up to the track on the other side may be a bit of a scramble. The house there is Frenchman's Creek Cottage, now restored by the Landmark Trust as holiday accommodation; this was once called Cuckoo Cottage, and in Chapter 8 of *The Helford River* Lady Vyvyan describes her time as part-owner of it, a haven of peace at a time when war was imminent.

Turn left on the track, and at the T-junction left again to walk down the path along the east side of Frenchman's Creek (*). Yes, somehow it is a slightly eerie place, where voices echo in the gloom, and the contorted white boughs and black, seaweed-festooned twigs of fallen trees look as if they have been half-buried in the mud for decades. Where the creek opens out a little you will see Withan Quay on the far side. The farm above that is Treveador. During the D-Day preparations in 1944, decoy lights were set up on the land of this farm and neighbouring Trelean to distract the attention of enemy aircraft from the actual centre of activities, at Trebah on the north side of the Helford. (See *Operation Cornwall*.)

After about half a mile the waterside path peters out, and you have to take the one on the right, up a few steps. Now you have fine open views, in strong contrast to the somewhat claustrophobic atmosphere below: the mouth of Frenchman's Creek, with an old quay, which once had pilchard cellars, on the far side; Groyne Point to the left; Calamansack and its woods ahead on the far side of the Helford.

FRENCHMAN'S CREEK

This place (also called Frenchman's Pill: "pill" means creek) inspired a short story by "Q" (Sir Arthur Quiller Couch) as well as Daphne du Maurier's famous novel. It's certainly easy to imagine smugglers landing booty here, and pirate-ships in hiding; indeed, the Helford as a whole was once nicknamed "Stealford": Richard Carew, the Tudor historian, wrote that "local pirates brought many a ship into the Helford creeks to plunder at leisure". No-one really knows how this creek got its name, but Oliver Padel has suggested that it could refer to a French ship. This brings to mind the fact that as part of the secret operations based on the Helford during World War II an imitation French trawler with powerful engines was prepared for action in the seclusion of Frenchman's Creek. (Again, see "Operation Cornwall".)

Near the head of Frenchman's Creek

❺ **A stile brings you to a lane; turn right, and continue on this for about a quarter of a mile.** Here there are glimpses to the left of the mouth of the Helford. **Ignore the first left turning, but after crossing a cattle-grid turn left, following the sign to Pengwedhen and Penarvon Cove; later, continue down the valley following the sign to Penarvon Cove.**

❻ *From the cove, you could if you wish do an attractive little round walk in the woods at Pengwedhen, which was presented to the National Trust in 1971. To find this, turn left by the "No parking on beach" sign. Where the track widens out in front of a house called "Penguin", a footpath is signposted on the left, up some steps. After passing among some buildings, look for the sign ahead, Woodland Circular Walk. The walk is easy to follow. Near the water's edge it brings you to the tiny St Francis' Chapel, built in 1930 in memory of a member of the family who owned Pengwedhen then; inside is a vivid statue of the saint.*

From Pengwedhen, return to the cove, cross the beach and take the path among the trees just beyond the stream. There are several Footpath signs to guide you into Helford. Turn left at the lane, then right into the village, entering it beside the Shipwright's Arms. Continue up the road beside the creek and over the footbridge to return to the car park.

WALKS 4 & 5

TWO WALKS BASED ON ST MARTIN

Walk 4, south from the church: under two miles.
Walk 5, to Colenso, Tremayne Quay and St Martin village: nearly five miles.
See also Footnote 1 on page 86.

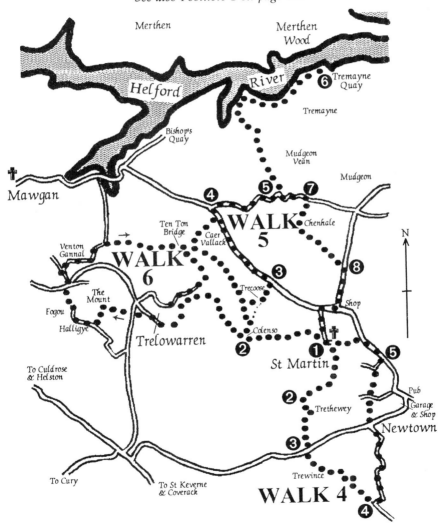

Walk 4 is a pleasant stroll through farming country on the edge of Goonhilly Downs. Near the start you are close to the dishes of the "Satellite Earth Station", and later there are wide views north-east to the coast. Most of the walk is on field-paths and farm tracks; about half a mile is along a very minor road, and near the end you are on a slightly busier road for a few hundred yards. A stick to deal with nettles at one stile could be helpful. There is no pub or shop on the route.

Walk 5 covers some of the same ground as the Trelowarren Woodland Walk (Walk 6). Between Easter and the end of September, this is an alternative worth considering; outside that period, the Trelowarrren walk is closed to the public. The route I am suggesting takes you from St Martin church across farmland down to the Trelowarren woods. When the Trelowarren walk is open, you can continue in the woods for the next mile or so, but otherwise there is a stretch of road to walk, normally very quiet out of season. After half a mile on a minor road you enter the woods above Tremayne, and there the National Trust has created or preserved a delightful walk down to the Quay, in some ways reminiscent of the Woodland Walk at Trelissick (part of Walk 4 in *Around the Fal*). From there you retrace your steps back to the road and walk to St Martin along quiet back-roads and paths. There are some quite steep hills, and a few patches in the woods were a tiny bit muddy even in the long, dry summer of 1989. The path near Chenhale Farm seems to be little-used, and you may have to climb some gates and duck under some barbed wire here. There is no pub on the route, but St Martin has a small shop.

To drive to St Martin church from Falmouth or Helston, follow the directions to Mawgan (Walk 7), continuing past Mawgan church for about two miles, ignoring the left turning to Helford and Manaccan. As you are entering St Martin, take the right turning signposted to the church. There is usually room there for several cars to park.

ST MARTIN IN MENEAGE CHURCH

Unless you have had a close look at the exterior, or have done some prior research, you will be surprised when you go in through the main door under the old tower to find yourself in what looks like a typical Nonconformist chapel. Previously there were a nave and aisles dating, like the tower, mainly from the 15th century, but in 1830 all except the tower was rebuilt, not - as at Redruth, for example - because of a need for increased accommodation, but following a disastrous fire.

St Martin was a 4th century Bishop of Tours in France (or, more accurately, Gaul), and there are other churches dedicated to him near Looe and on St Martin's island in the Scillies. In the 14th century, this church was rather mystifyingly called *"Sanctus Dydminus"* or *"Sanctus Martinus alias Dydemin"*. K.C.A.Wills explained this as from the Cornish phrase meaning *"homestead of two monks"*, and suggested that the monks might be St Mylor and St Anowe, both of whom seem to have had chapels nearby. Oliver Padel in *"Cornish Place Names"* (1988) assumes that the reference is to *"a completely unknown male saint."* As far as I know, nobody has suggested any connection with Ken Dodd.

St Martin parish is now officially linked with Manaccan, but until recently the church was, as Charles Henderson puts it, *"a chapelry to Mawgan"*. In 1381 the Pope granted permission for burials to take place at St Martin; before that, the dead had to be taken to St Mawgan, a journey involving two crossings of creeks and therefore sometimes impossible in those days.

St Martin-in-Meneage with Goonhilly beyond

WALK 4

❶ Walk down the lane on the right side of the church and turn right on to a footpath which goes downhill between hedges and soon reaches a stile and a footbridge over a stream. From here go straight up the centre of the field and then, as you approach the hedge, curve right to reach the top right-hand corner, crossing the stile a few paces to the right. The path now continues ahead almost directly towards the big dishes of the Goonhilly Satellite Earth Station (*) (though these are not visible at first), and with the hedge on the left.

GOONHILLY SATELLITE EARTH STATION

The construction of the first huge aerial began in 1961, and on 11 July 1962 Goonhilly became a household word in Britain when for the first time a live television picture from America was received on this side of the Atlantic, via the Telstar satellite. (A similar Earth Station in Brittany picked up the same signal.) That first aerial is nearly 26 metres across and weighs 1,100 tons; now there are ten aerials, some relatively small but others even larger than the original one. The largest of all, nearly 100 feet in diameter, was featured on a well-known TV programme when it was officially opened in the early '80s, and is nicknamed "Blue

Peter". *Nowadays, to quote from the colourful poster which you can buy at the public entrance, "Tens of millions of messages flow through Goonhilly every year; telephone calls, data and facsimile transmissions, television signals."*

For visitors there are a shop, a restaurant, a museum with audio-visual show, plus a conducted tour of the whole site by bus. These are available from Easter to mid-October, every day including Sundays, between 10 a.m. and 6 p.m.; for a visit to be fully worthwhile you would need to arrive by about 4.30. On the other hand, even if you have no wish to tour the site, to come here is always worthwhile because of the very special qualities of the landscape of Goonhilly Downs and the dramatic contrast between modern technology and the prehistoric remains that surround it. (Although it's no more than a mile in a straight line from point 4 in Walk 4, the road is much less direct than the proverbial crow and also carries fast traffic, so I'd recommend you to drive rather than extend the walk.)

❷ At the gate, turn left. A second gate brings you to the attractive buildings of Trethewey farm, and here you follow the drive on the right, which brings you to a road.

❸ Go right for a few yards, and then cross the low stone stile or cattle-grid on the left. Now walk with the hedge on your left, go through a gateway, and turn left and then immediately right on the main track leading to Trewince Farm. When you reach two wooden gates ahead, go through the left one and continue straight ahead with the hedge on your right. This brings you to a stile - rather awkward to climb, I'm afraid, and somewhat overgrown with nettles when we were last there.

❹ Turn left on this narrow little road, from which you get good views on a clear day. After rather more than half a mile you will reach a T-junction; continue straight ahead, over the stile, and keep beside the hedge on your left. The village on your right now is Newtown. (The maps add "-in-St Martin", but the locals call it just Newtown.) In fact it is quite old, but presumably developed later than St Martin itself. The use of "town" to mean village or farmstead is quite common in Cornwall - compare Leedstown and Charlestown, as well as the many "churchtowns". **The next stile brings you to a farm track leading to Haliggye farm,** whose name refers to willow-trees; the same name is found near the fogou on the Trelowarren walk. **Cross this track to another stile and continue as before. Soon the path becomes a track between hedges. A further stile beside a gateway leads to a wider track** (this one leads to Barrimaylor farm - a name which indicates that St Mylor was buried there, or at least had a chapel); **turn right on this track.**

❺ At the road, turn left. Soon you pass the Methodist Church, dated 1902; but notice that the house opposite was also once a nonconformist chapel (1839), and I suppose this is more likely to be the one mentioned by Jill Newton in *The Lizard*, although she attaches no date to her story: "I later discovered Customs men had searched the old manor at Mudgeon and found smuggled goods concealed there. The goods were confiscated and the owner of the house transported. Other free-traders suspected the Methodists of informing on this occasion and retaliated by breaking all the St Martin Chapel windows." (See Walk 3 for a note on Mudgeon.) **After about another 200 yards, don't miss the stile on the left. The path from here leads straight across the field to a stile just to the left of the church.**

WALK 5

❶ Walk back a little way along the road leading to the church, and turn left, crossing a stile. Go straight across the field to the next stile, and then along the farm lane slightly to the left of straight ahead. Cross the stile on the right of the farm gate, and continue straight down towards the trees at the lowest point of the field. The path down into the woods curves right and reaches a stream beside a house called Colenso, said in the Trelowarren walk leaflet to have been "probably the gamekeeper's cottage". "It has remained largely unchanged with no electricity, telephone or mains water," says the leaflet, but some modernisation seemed to be in progress in 1989. Mr Alan Bean of Trecoose tells me that the 1841 census shows Colenso to have been in use as a school then. He suggests that the name Colenso may derive from the Cornish, *kelly hinsow*, "the grove with the footpaths"; A.L.Rowse gives its meaning as "a dark pool by a wall or hedge".

❷ Don't cross the bridge but turn up to the right. Almost immediately, leave this lane, taking the path on the left, indicated as a public footpath by a yellow arrow. After about 250 yards of uphill walking the path or track levels off, and it is at this point that the two routes diverge.

If the Trelowarren Woodland Walk is open, the best route is to continue ahead, keeping within the woods for the next mile-or-so. Just before the track enters a clearing with timber-stacks and a static caravan, you could turn sharp left to Ten Ton Bridge, where there is an attractive little picnic area by the stream. For Tremayne Quay, go past the caravan on the track that curves uphill to the right. After about a quarter of a mile this reaches the road. Now continue with the directions from point 4.

If the Woodland Walk is closed (October to Easter), turn sharp right, following another yellow arrow. A gate admits you to the garden of Trecoose; please respect the owner's request to keep dogs on leads. The pretty garden is embellished with several statues and carvings, all the work of the owner. The path rejoins the lane coming up from Colenso; turn left on that, past Trecoose house, and soon you reach the road.

❸ Turn left, and keep to this road for about half a mile. Please take care, because the traffic can be fast on this fairly straight stretch. The farm on the right is Caervallack, named from a nearby small circular fort or settlement which probably dates from just before the Roman occupation. There is no public access to Caer Vallack, but it is visible on the left at a farm gate, marked by a ring of pines on an embankment. It is one of several such ancient rounds in this area: the largest is just a few hundred yards further along the road at Gear farm, whose name is another version of "Caer".

❹ Take the first turning on the right, a very narrow road which goes to Helford and Manaccan, but is not signposted.

(For those who have been on the Woodland Walk route: cross the "main" road and take the minor one almost opposite.)
After a while this descends to a wooded valley.

❺ Turn left on to the track with a National Trust sign, "Tremayne Quay". Ignore the side-paths to left and right as you descend through the woods beside the creek called Vellan Tremayne (meaning Tremayne Mill) towards the Helford itself. Where the track emerges from the trees for a while at the headland, the side path on the left leads down to the foreshore, affording a fine view up-river past the boathouse to where a gaggle of small boats cluster off Helford village. On the hilltop above this spot are the remains of another ancient earthwork. The large area of trees on the far side of the river is Merthen Wood, and on the hilltop can just be glimpsed Merthen Manor (*). Eventually the track reaches Tremayne Quay (*).

MERTHEN

The name comes from the Cornish, merthyn, a sea-fort, and the maps show the remains of a large earthwork on the hill above the woods, an ideal defensive position with an outlook across Groyne Point all the way to the mouth of the river. Merthen Manor is listed in the Domesday Book, and "The Lords of Merthen claimed jurisdiction over the whole river and creeks above a line drawn from Calamansack to Mainbroath Rock" (Henderson) - that is, roughly speaking, everything west of Port Navas and Helford village. Merthen became part of the Trelowarren estate early in the 17th century, and a branch of the Vyvyan family still lives there.

The oak wood was once part of a much larger one: Domesday records it as 1 league long and 1½ leagues wide - about 3½ by 5 miles. From the opposite bank it may look like virgin forest, but in fact it was coppiced, mainly for the production of charcoal, for at least three centuries (16th to 18th .... and there is documentary evidence of coppicing in nearby Calamansack woods as early as 1249). The charcoal was required for the blowing-houses which smelted the tin from the Wendron mines. Merthen Quay, now in ruins, was once busy with boats collecting charcoal or oysters or delivering limestone to the kilns there.

There were other lime-kilns at Bishop's Quay, near Mawgan, and at Gweek. Traditionally the acid soils of Cornwall had been improved by the application of sand from beaches and "towans" (dunes), but from the 15th century onwards limestone from South Wales and near Plymouth began to be shipped in and burnt, using charcoal or cheap coal, in kilns to prepare it for use in building and on the land. By the end of the 18th century there were hundreds of lime-kilns around the Cornish coasts. They were usually built into a bank so that alternate layers of coal and limestone could be loaded from above. Beneath was an arched opening, where the lime-burner would rake out the burnt quicklime, which would then be slaked with water and carted away. After the middle of the 19th century, lime-kilns gradually fell out of use, largely because burnt lime was superseded as a fertiliser by crushed limestone brought in by the railways.

Tremayne Quay with Merthen Wood beyond

In the 18th and 19th centuries, Merthen Quay was the highest point that the Norwegian timber ships could reach, so the logs were taken from here to Gweek by barges - again mainly for use in the mines.

There is no right of public access to the Merthen estate. (I was about to add, "unfortunately", but I'm in two minds about that.) The best way I know to capture the atmosphere of actually being there is to read Lady Vyvyan's book, "The Helford River", especially Chapter 4. For more detail about the history of Merthen Manor, see "The Story of the Vivians" by Stanley Vivian (1989).

TREMAYNE QUAY

"Mayne", as in "Maenporth", refers to stone; perhaps there was once a standing stone here - that would not be very surprising, since there is yet another ancient earthwork close by; but it could merely mean that the farmers found the land very stony, a fact which the present owner of Tremayne House confirms. Presumably there has been a landing-place at Tremayne for a very long time, with a track linking it to Caer Vallack and Trelowarren. In 1846, Queen Victoria and Prince Albert planned to visit Sir Richard Vyvyan at Trelowarren, so he had the quay we now see built to receive the Royal Yacht. In the event, bad weather caused the visit to be cancelled, and the Queen sent a marble bust of herself as a consolation. At last, in 1921, the Quay did receive a royal visitor: a photograph in Jill Newton's "Bygone Helston and the Lizard" shows Sir Courtenay Vyvyan receiving the Prince of Wales at the top of the steps.

❻ When you are ready to return up the track, it is worth taking the path on the right after a few yards. It runs along the edge of the bank and leads to the very solid and impressive but rather dilapidated boathouse. From there, the path above goes back to the main track via a few steps. Now return to the road by the same route as you came down on, except that when you reach the end of the section by water there is an attractive short diversion to the right which you could take, a side-path which goes down to a small slate footbridge at the head of Vellan Tremayne creek. Between the bridge and the creek is a small basin where the stream water was formerly dammed, perhaps as a fish trap or pond. **From the bridge the path curves back to the main track. At the road, turn left. The road winds up out of the valley for a few hundred yards.**

❼ *(The next section on footpaths is not particularly attractive, and the path is rather neglected, so you may prefer to stay on the road, taking the first right turn, and picking up the directions again at point 8.)*
Soon after passing the entrance to Mudgeon Vean farm, go through the six-bar metal gate on the right, on to a farm track. After a second gate the track curves left and reaches Chenhale Farm - rather dilapidated buildings in a junk-filled yard. Beyond the buildings is another gate,

which you will probably have to climb, and then duck under a strand of barbed wire. Go straight across the field to another metal farm gate - more climbing to do, I'm afraid! Still continue in the same direction for a little way, and then curve right near an impressive dung-heap (if it's still there), passing a house called Goondiwindi before reaching the road.

❽ **Turn right, and soon you are in St Martin village.** At the T-junction, notice the objects displayed in front of the house opposite. One looks like a mill-wheel, but we were told that both that and the contraption behind it were used in the process of fitting metal tires to wooden wheels. Turn left here if you want to visit the shop, but **to return to the church take the footpath to the right of the house I have just referred to.**

WALK 6
THE TRELOWARREN WOODLAND WALK

A choice of routes, about one-and-a-half to six miles.
For the sketch map, see the start of Walk 4.

Most of this walk lies within the Trelowarren estates, by permission of Sir John Vyvyan, and is open to the public only between the start of April and the end of September; the section from Caer Vallack to Tremayne Quay, however, can be walked at any time. The main circular route is marked with yellow arrows or blobs of paint. A handy leaflet about the walk can be bought at Trelowarren; this includes an O.S. map and notes on points of interest. In theory, therefore, all I need do now is leave you to enjoy the walk, but in practice I think I can contribute something useful, especially since the leaflet is not always available. Even with the leaflet, you might be glad of occasional help in finding the way, and a few extra notes.

The walk crosses farmland at first, and in this section there is a good viewing-point and also a site of special archaeological interest: take a torch with you to explore inside the fogou. Nearly all the rest of the route is in woodland, very beautiful and peaceful. There were only a few muddy patches when we were there, despite recent heavy rain. The hills are not steep, but some are long. Refreshments are on sale at Trelowarren: the licensed "Bistro" serves a good range of snacks and full meals.

To drive to Trelowarren (*), follow the directions as given for Mawgan (Walk 7), as far as the war memorial; then, instead of turning left, go straight on towards Garras, and soon Trelowarren is signposted on the left. The walk starts at the car park on the right just before you reach the house.

TRELOWARREN

The Manor of Trelowarren (sometimes explained as meaning "fox farm", but Oliver Padel rejects that theory) seems to have belonged to the Earls of Wessex before the Norman Conquest. It then passed to the new king's half-brother, the Count of Mortain. "And it is worth 15s," states Domesday Book, "and when the Count received it, it was worth 30s." Readers of Daphne du Maurier's "The House on the Strand" will be familiar with the names of the Cardinham and Ferrers families, who owned it successively from the 13th century until 1427 when John Vyvyan of Trevedran near Penzance married Honora Ferrers. The Vyvyans remain the owners to this day.

The oldest part of Trelowarren House seems to date from John's time there; this is the east wing, which faces you as you come along the main drive. Part of the chapel also dates from then, but it was extended in "Gothick" style about 1750-

60. *The stables and several other parts of the house were built late in the 17th century, and the Victorian era saw further extensions and rebuildings. The Folk Museum at Helston is one of the best in the County, and its most impressive exhibit is a huge wooden cider press which was in use at Trelowarren between about 1750 and 1920. The stone apple-crusher is also on display there.*

Delightful personal accounts of life at Trelowarren some forty to eighty years ago are to be found in the writings of Lady C.C.Vyvyan, notably "The Helford River" and "The Old Place".

Part of Trelowarren house is now used as a retreat run by an interdenominational Christian fellowship. Each year a series of chamber concerts and recitals is held in the chapel and adjacent library. The house is open to the public for visits on certain days: to check arrangements for the current year, please ring 01326-221224. At the same time you could find out about opening times of the Craft Centre (the former stables, now adopted by the Cornwall Crafts Association), the Pottery and the Bistro. The last is in the old coach-house.

The route is clearly signposted as far as "The Mount", the mound on your right, which is worth climbing for the fine views towards Mount's Bay and Mawgan church. The Mount is thought to have been created last century with earth excavated for a new drive which was never actually completed. **From there, turn left and walk along the field-edge as far as the track; turn right on that**, and this brings you to the thatched cottages at Halligye or Halliggye ("willows"). **The arrows direct you right, down to a stile. After crossing that, turn left and go through the kissing-gate** to inspect the impressive fogou (*).

A cottage at Halligye

HALLIGYE FOGOU

Between about 200BC and 400AD there seem to have been many fortified settlements around the Helford, and the high ground at Halligye was evidently the site for one of them. Traces of a rampart and ditch remain. This fogou, 90 feet long and 6 feet high (but not all the way, so watch your head!), is the largest in England and Wales and very well preserved, although obviously a good deal of reconstruction has been done: the existing entrance, for example, is new. The leaflet assumes that this fogou was for defensive purposes, and paints a gruesome picture of attackers' heads and/or feet being lopped off; but fogous may have had a religious function, or been built merely as stores or cold larders. In "Journey to the Stones" and "Mother and Sun", Ian Cooke gives detailed accounts of fogous and argues that they were related to sun-worship. The word is derived from the Cornish "ogo", a cave.

Now the walk continues downhill by the hedge on the right, where you turn left and immediately right, following this drive as it bears right to two more pretty thatched cottages and an impressive old drinking-trough at Venton Gannal ("spring or well with a channel"). Don't miss the stile on the right soon after, and a few yards later go left past a tall wooden "itching post" and down to a stile (both these are marked with yellow paint). Ignore the side path on the left beyond the stile. After about half a mile, another prominent track comes in from the right.

Here you could turn right for a short cut back to Trelowarren; otherwise, go straight on, and soon you reach Ten Ton Bridge, with its pretty little picnic site by the stream. Beyond this, a yellow arrow directs you to turn right: this is the continuation of the circular walk via Colenso, an isolated house which was probably once the gamekeeper's cottage. There, you cross the footbridge, turn right, then climb a few steps (yellow arrow) on to the attractive footpath that leads back to the house. However, if you want to include a visit to Tremayne Quay on this walk, adding about three miles to the distance, ignore the right turning just past Ten Ton Bridge; continue through the clearing containing an old caravan, and bear right on the uphill track. In about a quarter of a mile this brings you to the road close to the ancient site of Caer Vallack. From there, follow the directions given for Walk 5, starting at point 4, but at the end of point 6 turn right at the road, returning to Trelowarren by the same route as far as the Ten Ton Bridge area. From there you could proceed via Colenso or take the shorter route back beyond the bridge, as mentioned earlier. For notes on Merthen and Tremayne Quay, see Walk 5.

WALK 7
MAWGAN AND GWEEK
Nearly four miles.

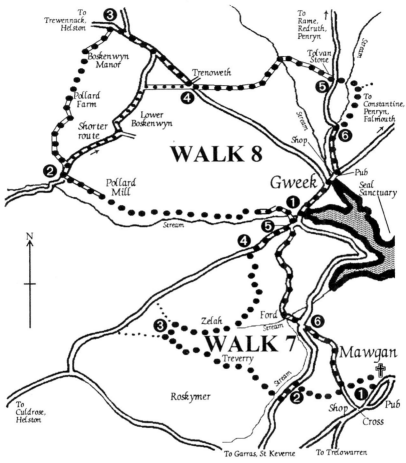

Mawgan in Meneage is an attractive village in a beautiful area. Unfortunately for walkers, the banks of the Helford between Mawgan Creek and Gweek are privately owned and have no public footpaths. The walk suggested here, therefore, gives you no glimpse of the river unless you choose to go into Gweek village; instead it alternates between woods and undulating farmland with extensive views. Because one section of footpath has become unusable, I have had to include a short stretch of road which is often busy, leading down into Gweek. Almost the whole of the return half of the walk is on road, but it is a quiet and most attractive one.

The rest of the route is mostly on well-surfaced tracks, but the narrower footpaths through woodland and over fields may require waterproof footwear, and one or two places were rather "nettly and brambly" when I was last there. There are some quite steep hills. Mawgan village has a shop and a pub; so, too, has Gweek, but to walk to them would add over half a mile to the distance. Mawgan in Meneage shares with Mawgan in Pydar the mixed blessing of being close to a busy airfield, so to appreciate fully the quietness of the woods and fields it may be best to choose a Sunday for this walk.

To drive to Mawgan from Falmouth, take the Gweek road (B3291). On leaving Gweek, take the first left turn, and continue for about two miles till you reach a war memorial at a crossroads. Here turn left, and when you reach Mawgan continue along the main road to the church. There are parking spaces on the right just before the church. From Helston, drive south on the A3083 Lizard road; after passing RNAS Culdrose, turn left on to the B3293. After about three miles this brings you to the war memorial; here turn left, following the sign to Mawgan.

ST MAWGAN CHURCH

The patron saint, Maugan, is also commemorated at Mawgan Porth and St Mawgan, east of Newquay: a Welsh Abbot and Bishop, he crossed Cornwall in the 6th century en route for Brittany, landing at Porth and setting sail again from Mawgan Creek. He probably founded the original church here, but the oldest parts of the surviving building date from the 13th century. It was greatly altered and enlarged in the 15th, and the beautifully carved wagon roof in the north aisle was built then. Among the many points of interest are the "peephole" or squint which gives a view of the altar from the south transept; the tomb, helmet and sword of Sir Richard Vyvyan of Trelowarren (died, 1665), who was in command of the Royalist forces at Dennis Head during the Civil War: see Walk 2; and in the Lady Chapel the stone effigies of a knight and his lady. The Rev. Peter Long's interesting leaflet about the church states that these represent Sir Roger de Carminow and his wife, and that he was a descendant of King Arthur and a crusader during the reign of Edward I. The home of the Carminows was further west, near Loe Bar, and the effigies were brought to Mawgan from the chapel there early in the 17th century. (The Carminows form the link with "The House on the Strand": see the start of the church leaflet.) The last main alterations to the church were made in 1894. The photographs at the west end may well have been intended as evidence of the great improvements made then, but John Betjeman's comment is, "Photographs hang to show how lovely it once was."

❶ From the church (*) return along the road for a few yards and turn right up the drive to Gwarth-an-Drea (meaning "the upper farm"); this runs beside the churchyard. A little way up, just past the entrance drive to a new bungalow, turn left where there is a yellow waymark arrow. The path runs on the left side of the hedge. Just beyond the bungalow, cross the rough stile and continue along the right-hand side of the field, which gives attractive open views. Goonhilly Satellite Earth Station is now quite close, on the left. A stile brings you to a road. Go slightly left to the next stile. Now the path runs straight down the centre of the field to a gate, and the track beyond that leads to a second gate and another road. (This one can be busy, so take care.)

❷ Cross the road, turn left, and after a few yards take the footpath signposted on the right, which takes you down a few steps into the wood and then runs beside a stream. Ignore the side path to the left: cross the footbridge and then go gently uphill on a wide track close to the edge of the wood. At Treverry Farm continue on the main track between house and farm buildings (the latter apparently being converted into living accommodation when we were there), and on past a friendly white kitten with one blue eye and one green. (I apologise if the kitten has moved by the time you do this walk.) By now the track has become a surfaced drive or road, and it passes a small Ministry of Defence area with masts, presumably associated with Culdrose airfield.

❸ At the sign to Zelah Farm turn sharp right, via a metal gate, and now continue on this driveway past Zelah - not a Cornish name, by the way, but derived from an Old English word for a hall - and Higher Trevilgen (the attractive footpath going south-east from here is now, sadly, impassable because of barbed wire, brambles and bogs) until eventually you reach the B3291 road from Gweek to Culdrose.

❹ Turn right, and please go carefully on this road: the traffic can be speedy. Luckily, it's not too far to Gweek, and all downhill.

❺ On the edge of Gweek is the Old Corn Mill, converted into flats in the late 1970s. Until then there were two large, interconnected grist mills. The 25-foot-diameter waterwheel still in place was erected here in 1905, but the buildings in essence are about 200 years old, and written records of milling on this site go back to 1432. (For an interesting article about "Lower Gweek Mills" by Anthony Hitchens Unwin, see *The Journal of the Trevithick Society*, No. 10, 1983. Six photographs dating from before the conversion are included. One photograph and brief information about "Gweek Mill" can be found in *An Introduction to Cornish Watermills* by D.E.Benney, Bradford Barton 1972.)

To explore the village, details about which are given in Walk 8, continue along the main road; but for the walk back to Mawgan turn sharply to your right up the narrow road opposite the Mill. The road, which is not signposted apart from a sign to Gweek House, goes steeply uphill at first, then brings you down to a ford at a pretty spot in the woods.

*The bridge
by the ford*

❻ Just beyond this, cross the wider road and continue up the narrow one as it again climbs steeply among the trees. After less than half a mile you will reach the two stiles at the point where you crossed this road before; here you could either turn left and retrace your steps, or continue along the road to the ancient inscribed stone known as Mawgan Cross at the crossroads in Mawgan village, turning left there to return to your car.

MAWGAN CROSS   (Photo on back cover.)

Mawgan Cross is in fact only a shaft; a socket at the top suggests there was once a cross head. On the shaft are cut the words "Cnegvmi fili Genaivs" ("Cnegumus son of Genaius"). The style of the lettering indicates that it was inscribed at least four centuries after the Roman occupation; the use of Roman names at so late a date gives the impression that Cornwall was well behind the times even then. Long may it continue that way!

The pub, which serves a wide range of snacks and meals, is signposted near the cross: it is on the minor road that loops to the south of the main one and re-joins it just past the church. Formerly called The Ship, it is now The Old Court House, and the restaurant area is a mock-up of a little courtroom. Suspects were once tried in a back-room of The Ship, and public hangings took place at Traboe Cross, about three miles to the south - the point at which the boundaries of five parishes meet.

WALK 8

A WALK BASED ON GWEEK

About four and a half miles. For the sketch map, see the start of Walk 7.

Apart from roads - mostly quite busy - there is no public right of way along either side of the Helford at the Gweek end for quite a long distance: most of the land either belongs to the Trelowarren estate or has been sold by the estate to other private owners. Luckily, there are some good inland walks from Gweek, and this is one I particularly recommend. Two streams enter the Helford at Gweek; the walk starts by following the course of one of them up a pretty valley, then cuts across farming country before coming down to one of the two valleys which feed water to the second stream. Finally the third valley is reached, and from there the path follows that stream back to Gweek. A walk of this sort is more of an adventure than most in this book. There is almost certain to be plenty of mud, especially around the streams: in three or four places wellies were essential when I last walked the route, in the wet January of 1995. When you are crossing farmland on little-used paths you have to be prepared for barbed wire, electric fences, overgrown stiles, ploughed fields and so on. Please don't be frightened off, though, because when my wife and I first did this walk we met with few problems apart from the mud and getting lost a few times, and I trust that the following directions will help you avoid the second of those. The whole walk is "out in the wilds", far from shops and pubs once you leave Gweek. There is no steep hill along the way. Gweek itself is well worth a close look: too many people see it only from their car windows or stop only at the Seal Sanctuary.

To drive to Gweek from Falmouth or Penryn, take the B3291 from near Penryn Bridge. From Helston, go south on the Lizard road (A3083), turning left just past RNAS Culdrose on to the St Keverne road (B3293) and then left again on to the B3291 to Gweek. Public parking is not plentiful in the village, but any suitable space you can find between the two bridges would be convenient for the walk. The Gweek Stores / Post Office has a small car park for customers, so why not be one? The pasties on sale there were praised in a very perceptive article in "The Guardian" - which, incidentally, also recommended "Around the Helford"!

GWEEK
Only a short distance from the route of Walk 8 are the earthworks at Grambla (near Boskenwyn) and Carwythenack (east of Tolvan). There is evidence that both

were Roman camps; ridgeways link them to Gweek, and the likelihood that Gweek was a Roman trading port is reinforced by its name if you accept the theory that it derives from the Latin "vicus", a town. Oliver Padel thinks it is more likely to come from Celtic words for forest or village, and others are confident that it derives from "wyk", meaning "creek".

Gweek Quay

In any case there can be no doubt that this has been a port for many centuries; like Tregony on the Fal, it offered a haven comparatively safe from gales and pirates. Its importance grew when Helston's access to Mount's Bay was cut off by Loe Bar. A document of 1301 records two gallows at "Wike", one set up by Roger de Carminow of Winianton Manor, and the other by the burgesses of Helston, seeking to protect their shipping interests in what was now the town's port. The shipping of tin from Gweek goes back a long way - some suggest as far as 450 BC - and there were two ancient blowing-houses (for smelting tin) in the village. According to A.S.Oates, primitive stone tin-moulds are built into the quay walls. The mining, and especially tin-streaming, eventually caused the silting which now makes it so hard to imagine big ships reaching Gweek. Timber had to be floated up-river or barged from Merthen; it was then stored till needed in a large pond by one of the bridges. But quite large cargo vessels continued to make their way up to Gweek as recently as the 1930s; Lane's "Guide to the Helford" (1890) describes "coasters lying high and dry, discharging coals, bricks, tiles and other like merchantise, with masts and yards embroidered in the overhanging

foliage," and members of the crews "on the end of the topsail yard, picking some
fruit from the neighbouring branch of an apple tree."

Today Gweek is still quite busy, with a trade in (for example) earthenware as
well as the more expected activities involved in the building and repair of boats.
The earthenware makers at the Odyssey Trading Post have recently (late 1994)
begun "capturing" strange beings known as Livingstones (Biolithos Cornubiensis) -
go and see! A long-defunct maritime museum on the quay has left behind a replica
pirate ship made for a film; beside it are picnic tables and a coffee shop serving
light refreshments every day except Sundays throughout the year (9-5 except
Saturdays, 10-4). Those interested in boats might like to inspect the Bristol
Channel Pilot Cutter which is being restored; I am told it should be here at least
till 1999.

A literary footnote: In "Hereward the Wake" (1866), Kingsley tells "How
Hereward succoured a Princess of Cornwall" - twice. Gweek was the setting for
these deeds. Hereward and his companions "sailed in .... up a tide river which
wandered and branched away inland like a tide-locked lake, between high green
walls of oak and ash, till they saw at the head of the tide Alef's town .... He went
up .... past the ugly dykes and muddy leats, where Alef's slaves were streaming
the gravel for tin ore; through rich alluvial pastures spotted with red cattle; and up
to Alef's town." Hereward saved the Princess from having to marry Ironhook;
with a hint of prophecy, we hear that she "would as lief marry a seal"!

❶ **The walk starts near the southern bridge, that is, the second bridge if
you are approaching from the Falmouth direction. Take the track which
starts on the left of it (as you face inland). After passing the converted
mill buildings** (some details about Lower Gweek Mills are given near the
end of Walk 7), **on the left, it crosses the stream and then bears left to
follow the valley. Beyond the last houses (a little terrace of cottages with
their own telephone box), cross the stile on the right of a gate and walk
with the hedge on your right.** Notice how the stream has been dammed in
order to create the pool for Lower Gweek Mills. **Next you go through a
farm gate and then continue in the same line till you come to quite a
large field sloping down towards the stream. Now go diagonally down
to the fence at the bottom. The official footpath from here actually runs
along the left side of the hedge, inside the wooded patch, but if it's too
muddy and overgrown there you may have to keep to the field edge.
When a small stream cuts across your path, go left, over what's likely to
be a very boggy area, through a metal kissing-gate, and continue in the
same direction across the field to two farm gates. I don't know which is
the "official" one for walkers to use, but the further one is much the
easier to open, despite being off its hinges. Beyond that, you are on a
grassy track between hedges which eventually brings you to Pollard**

("high pool") Mill. This is attractively preserved or restored, with its wheel still in good condition and the leat clear all the way to the road.

❷ On reaching the road, first it's worth going left a few yards to the bridge, where you can see the sluice-gate by which the stream water can be diverted into the mill leat. To continue the walk, go back along the road, past the drive from Pollard Mill, and up the hill. Take the first left turning, which is a concrete drive leading to Pollard Farm, with beautiful views to the wooded valley on the left.

(But if you want to shorten the walk by about ½m., you could keep to the road for half a mile or so, taking the second track on the right, beyond Lower Boskenwyn Farm. This is shown on the sketch map. It brings you to point 4 in the directions.)

In the farmyard at Pollard Farm turn left past the house and haystore, then cross the field to a stile on the right of a double electricity-supply pole. If the patch beyond the stile is overgrown and festooned with barbed wire (as it has been for at least five years) you may have to climb the metal gate on the right. Now walk with the hedge on your left towards Boskenwyn ("home on the white ridge") Farm. Look back now for a wide view to the south including Culdrose airfield and the Satellite Earth Station and new windmills at Goonhilly Downs. Beyond the farm gateway - usually muddy - turn right on to the main track, which brings you after about a quarter of a mile to the road. There, unless it has been removed since January 1995, you will find a rather intriguing and elderly-looking contraption - perhaps a device for loading wagons (?).

❸ Turn right. Now follows a rather dull threequarter-mile-or-so of road walking, for which I apologise. You pass the school and continue towards Gweek; next comes Barton Farm, and finally Trenoweth ("new farm"), with Boskenwyn Chapel opposite.

❹ Just beyond this, take the track on the left (not the entrance drive to the farm), and go on down past the house into the valley. Ignore the turnings on the right. In the distance to the left notice a lone wind turbine (which I have never seen actually turning), and, further left, an engine house plus two or three mine chimney-stacks. These are relics of tin mines in the Wendron district: Trevenen, Trumpet Consols and others. As you approach the bottom of the slope you'll probably be glad you wore your boots, if you did. It's usually particularly muddy where the track runs beside the stream beyond the bridge. Continue up to the road at Tolvan Cross, where you may be able to catch a glimpse through or over the hedge on your left of the Tolvan Stone (*), in the back garden of the house on the corner.

THE TOLVAN STONE

"Tol-ven" in Cornish meant "holed stone", and such stones were regarded as having magic powers of healing. One Victorian antiquarian recorded the custom here of passing a sick child nine - some say seven - times through the hole and then letting it sleep on a nearby mound with a sixpence under its head. Lady Vyvyan in "The Helford River" tells how this "last surviving stone of a great circle" (not every archaeologist would accept that, by the way), had bits hacked off it in 1847 and was then re-erected, "squeezed into the back-yard of a cottage". She complains at the way it has been demeaned into a familiar domestic object: '"You are like a bird in a cage," I thought.' The hole may have been cut in granite slabs like this one and the Mên-an-Tol in West Penwith to act as a restricted entrance to a chamber tomb - large enough for offerings to be placed inside and for the

spirit of the dead to escape. But no such tombs are known nearby, and no chamber tombs with holed entrances have been found in Cornwall, although there are several in Europe. Ian Cooke, in "Journey to the Stones", writes of the pagan rites of fertility and healing associated with such stones, and also suggests that the holes may have been caused naturally by weather action.

The Tolvan Stone

❺ Cross the road and continue down the track opposite. After the footbridge beside the ford the track curves right; just before the left curve which follows, cross the stile on the right, next to a farm gate. Now for a short distance the course of the footpath is far from clear. It never deviates very far from the stream, but the patch beside the stream at first is marshy, so you need to go a little way up to the left to find a wooden farm gate. On the far side of it is a short stretch of grassy lane, with the ruins of a small building on the left. Once you emerge into an open space, the path is clear again, running quite near the stream - rather muddy but through very pretty country. There is a metal gate, then a grassy lane above Candron Water Farm (recently "diversified" as secondhand car dealers), and finally a wooden gate at the road.

❻ Turn left, and soon you enter Gweek. Tolkien addicts should not miss the Gweek Teagardens - or "The Hobbit Teagardens", as a friend of ours calls them. With the Mellanoweth ("new mill") Restaurant, the Black Swan, the Gweek Stores and the coffee shop on the quay also beckoning, those in need of refreshments are spoilt for choice. If you still have time and strength to spare, this would be a good opportunity to visit the Seal Sanctuary (*) and to explore Gweek itself.

THE CORNISH SEAL SANCTUARY

I vividly recall visits to Trevaunance Cove at St Agnes in the late 60s when I had just come to live in Cornwall, and my children's delight in watching the seals at the little sanctuary there. The story of Ken Jones's early retirement as a miner; his move, with his wife, to Cornwall; the first attempt they made to rescue a seal; and how from those small beginnings has developed this ambitious enterprise, including a special hospital as well as several large pools: all this is told in detail in his book, "Seal Doctor" (Fontana paperbacks). Early in 1973 the Cornish Seal Sanctuary was bought by Vardon PLC, a firm based in Wimborne, which operates Sea Life Centres at several other places in Britain, plus one in Holland. The Sanctuary is open to visitors every day except Christmas Day, from 9.00 to 5.30 (9.00 to 4.00 from October to Easter). To see the seals fed you should be there at 10.30, 11.30, 2.30 or 3.30; in the summer there are two extra feeding times, 12.30 and 4.30. There is a short "woodland trail" beside the creek, and guided nature-trail walks are available.

WALK 9

CONSTANTINE, POLWHEVERAL
& PORT NAVAS

About four and a half miles. With recommended diversions, about six miles.
See page 86 for a shorter walk omitting Port Navas.

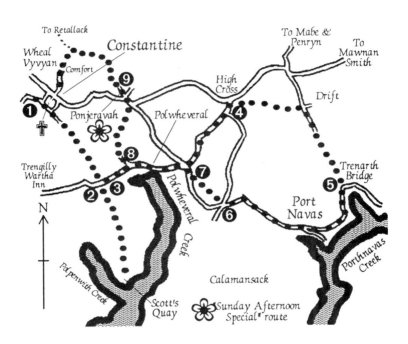

Considering that Constantine is one of the largest villages around the
Helford, and that Port Navas is one of the places most favoured by
yachtsmen and builders of superior retirement homes, it's surprising how
far from human habitation you can feel on much of this walk. This is
especially true of the walk to and from Scott's Quay, which is given here as
an optional extra; it could be done as a short independent walk, perhaps
starting and ending at the Trengilly Wartha Inn at Nancenoy. Scott's Quay
is probably most attractive at high water. Most of the main walk route is
inland, but there are frequent beautiful views of the river, and you do walk
beside the creeks at Port Navas and Polwheveral. The latter seems to me
one of those very special places which are enough in themselves to make

47

any walk worthwhile - and I do hope you will go there for the first time on foot rather than by car, which would rob it of some of its magic. Unfortunately, this area is not very rich in public footpaths, so I have had to include a couple of sections of road which you may find a bit dreary, especially the uphill slog out of Port Navas; on the other hand, the road between Trenarth Bridge and Port Navas has such fine views that I feel no need to apologise for sending you along it. Mud could well be thick on the ground, especially just above Scott's Quay: you'll definitely need your wellies if you attempt that part of the walk after a wet spell. Two good pubs are available: the Queen's Arms in Constantine and the Trengilly Wartha Inn at Nancenoy, which is about a quarter of a mile west of the walk route at its nearest point. I haven't sampled the food at the Queen's Arms, but can vouch for Trengilly Sausage. There are shops at Constantine but nothing in the way of refreshments at Port Navas unless you happen to be a member of the Yacht Club.

To drive to Constantine (*) from Falmouth, take the B3291 as directed for Walk 13, turning left at Lamanva or Brill; from Helston, follow the directions already given for Gweek (Walk 8), continuing along the B3291 to Brill, where you turn right. The car park is signposted along Vicarage Terrace, on the right if you are coming from Brill, close to the church. There are public toilets at the car park.

CONSTANTINE

The village's name - originally, but not now, pronounced as "Constenton" - is that of the saint to whom the church is dedicated, perhaps a 6th century King of Cornwall and Devon whose main claim to sainthood seems to have been that he murdered two princes at a church altar. Some say that he was later converted and "put away his sword". There is evidence of a Celtic monastery at Constantine before the Conquest, and of a Norman church after it.

The fine granite church we now see dates from the 15th century. Do go inside if you can; it's normally open from 9 till 4. The booklet on sale is one of the best of its type I have seen, and provides a much better guide to the church than I have space for. Just in case you're unable to find a copy, I'll point out the most famous object, which is set into the floor on the left side of the altar: the Gerveys Brass, which commemorates a man and his wife both buried on the same day in 1574, and portrays all their sixteen children in minute detail. The same brass had originally been part of a memorial to a Flemish knight two hundred years before; his portrait is on the reverse side, and you can see a framed rubbing of it on the wall above. In the north aisle are several other items of interest, including part of the original rood screen, a Henry VIII groat found in the churchyard wall, three old bell clappers dated 1809, two aerial photographs of the church, and the remains of a medieval wall painting just to the left of the wall tablet in memory of John Maule.

According to A.K.Hamilton Jenkin, Constantine consisted of only twenty houses in 1820, and he attributes its remarkable growth entirely to mining. The most important mine nearby was at Comfort, north of the church, with other workings in the valley below, and was named Wheal Vyvyan since it stood on land owned by the Vyvyans of Trelowarren (see Walk 6). Between 1827 and 1856 it sold over 8,000 tons of copper ore plus a small amount of tin, but by 1864 the best part of the "lode" or seam was worked out. At its busiest the mine employed about 120 people, 80 of them underground.

I always hesitate to question any statement made by Dr Hamilton Jenkin, but one must surely point out the great importance of the granite industry as a local employer, though admittedly this reached its peak rather later than the mines.

Those interested in knowing the history of Constantine parish in detail should seek out Charles Henderson's book on it - quite a rarity these days.

❶ From the car park, take the first right turning, passing the main entrance of the church. Where the road bears left, carry straight on along the minor road marked Bowling Green, passing the W.I. Hall. Soon the road becomes a path. Cross the granite stile beside the gate marked Polwartha ("above the pool or creek") **Farm, and go straight across the field - that is, gradually veering away from the field-edge on the right - down to the next stile, then in the same line to two more stiles.**

❷ At the road, you have choices to make: turn right for the Trengilly Wartha Inn; turn left for the main circular walk, following the directions from point 3; or go straight ahead for Scott's Quay.

Heading for Scott's Quay: **At the next gate there is a ladder-stile to climb. From there it is simply a matter of continuing ahead along farm track or footpath, through a patch of woodland** - probably lots of mud to contend with there, I'm afraid - **and out on to the peninsula bordered by Polpenwith and Polwheveral Creeks till you come down to the delightful Scott's Quay (*) with its tiny beach.** I suspect you will want to linger there. When you finally feel you must go, **return to the road by the same route and turn left for the pub or right for the circular walk.**

SCOTT'S QUAY

I am grateful to Mrs Vanessa Beeman for the information that a local lawyer, Charles Scott, had this quay built, some time quite early last century. He was unpopular in his lifetime, and perhaps is little better liked now, since his ghost on horseback is said to haunt a lane near Brill. (This is close to Trewardreva, where a descendant of his, Sir Peter Scott, used to live.) A variation on this story is that Scott's ghost used to gallop through Constantine village, followed by his hounds.

Constantine parish was once famous for the granite it exported all round the world. A lot of it was shipped from Penryn, but Scott's Quay was also used for that purpose; in fact, according to Liz Luck ("South Cornish Harbours") it was "the main shipping point" and as a result Polwheveral Creek became "a great artery of trade" during the 19th century. See the later note on Port Navas, however, for further discussion of what was the main local shipping point for granite. It seems probable that Wheal Vyvyan and the other mines around Constantine would also have employed the quay to ship copper ore for smelting and to obtain supplies of coal and timber.

❸ As you descend the pretty road towards Polwheveral (*), the sound of rushing water fills the air long before you see the stream tumbling over rocks beside the old house at the head of the creek.

Polwheveral Bridge, shrouded among trees

POLWHEVERAL

The name seems to mean "creek with the lively stream"; another possibility is "February creek", an interpretation calling for some creative imagination. The attractive little granite bridge was built in 1572: the contract between the parish and the mason, Roger Hallard of Tregony, for the building of the bridge still survives. He received £3 6s 8d (£3.33) for the work, which also included clearing the approach roads of all rocks and stones, and maintaining the bridge for the rest of his life. The lively stream and an occasional car are all that break the silence now, but once the stream here powered a Cornish Stamps machine, which crushed the ore from Wheal Vyvyan. A short way south-east of Polwheveral there was an iron mine called Wheal Brogden, which seems to have worked mainly during the 1870s; a lucrative tin-streaming enterprise operated in the valley after Wheal Vyvyan closed down; and the former Vicar of Constantine, the Rev. Vincent Holyer, informed me that there are two adits (drainage shafts) of an old tin mine between the road and the creek, but I have not found any written evidence to confirm this. Charles Henderson's history of Constantine mentions a tucking or fulling mill (for cleaning woollen cloth) at Polwheveral, and also two grist mills. He tells the story of Henwood, one of the millers, who was a widower with a daughter. When he planned to re-marry, some Constantine men disapproved, saying that it was his duty to devote himself to his daughter, and "burnt him in effigy at his own door."

Going up the road on the other side, you have a view of the creek itself. At the crossroads go straight on - an uphill stretch between high hedges. In the first edition of this book I called it "rather boring", but the lady who told me about Charles Scott also pointed out that this lane is a profusion of wild flowers in spring and summer. "Also," she added, "it is one of the most ancient crossroutes - known as Clodgy Lane, like the one in Helston - and could tell a few tales!" ("Clodgy" might refer to a lazar-house, but in this case is more likely to mean "sticky".) One point of interest is the ultra-modern-looking house on the left, which has been featured on local television as a pioneering and apparently successful attempt to make maximum use of solar energy. A little later, another example of modern technology, this time harnessing wind-power, can be seen on the skyline ahead. This windmill supplies enough electricity for the farm it's on and also some over for sale to SWEB.

Ignore the right turning, and continue a little further to the T-junction at High Cross.

❹ **Go over the stile on the right (there is a public footpath sign), cross the field to another stile, then go straight on across the next field to a further stile between granite posts. Still continue in the same line past the right-hand tree to yet another stile in the corner, where there is a** second footpath sign. Go on down to the trees, and a few yards to the right there is a granite stile; to reach it, I'm afraid you'll have to cross a very sticky patch bordering a small stream. Bear right on the path, and when you reach a drive keep straight on, among some Monterey pines. Turn left by the bungalow, cross the stile and turn right. Keep straight on where the main track goes left to Trenarth Manor (see the note in Walk 10), and again straight on where the lesser track turns right, and yet again straight on where the hedge turns left. Now go to the corner of the field, where a gap leads into woodland; you may have to duck under some barbed wire. From here, follow the pleasant valley path down to Trenarth Bridge.

❺ Turn right. The road can be busy in summer, but for some of the way you can keep clear of traffic by walking on the bank on the creek side. Eventually, after passing several modern houses with enviable views down the creek, you descend to the older waterside cottages of Port Navas (*), and can turn left along the road beside the little inlet, lined with private quays. Near the end is Old Kiln; for facts about lime-kilns see the note on Merthen (Walk 5). **Continue to the left of the Yacht Club entrance** to find the scene shown at the front of the book: Porthnavas Creek, nicknamed "Abraham's Bosom" in Lady Vyvyan's "The Helford River". Beside the quay are the buildings of the Duchy of Cornwall Oyster Farm, where oysters are usually on sale. The oyster beds in the creek are marked with tall sticks.

PORT NAVAS

It's "Porth Navas" on the maps, but the h is usually dropped now. "Cove of the sheep" is Dr Padel's explanation: if he is right, the name dates from times when agriculture was the mainstay. A more appropriate name now might be "cove of the yachtsman" or "cove of the oyster".

Oyster farming in Cornwall dates at least from Roman times; some say that the Romans introduced oysters to the Fal and the Helford. For many centuries, the rights of fishery and oysterage in the Helford River were claimed by the Lords of Merthen west of Calamansack and by the Lords of Manaccan - namely, the Bishops of Exeter - to the east. Later the Bishops' interest passed to the Duchy of Cornwall, and in about 1930 Edward Duke of Cornwall (later Edward VIII), hoping to reduce unemployment in the area, bought the upper rights from the Vyvyan family, then (as now) Lords of Merthen. This eventually led to the establishment of the Duchy of Cornwall Oyster Farm, which for many years was controlled directly by the Duchy but is now leased out. Oysters are brought from other beds in the Helford and Fal and relaid at the Oyster Farm to purify and fatten. The business thrived, but in recent years has been seriously threatened by a killer disease, Bonamia, which had previously been found only in the Pacific.

Around the start of this century, Port Navas was one of the main ports for shipping blocks of granite: "Immense numbers of these blocks," says a contemporary account, "are piled up to forty or fifty feet in height, waiting to be loaded into the two or three ketches, schooners or smacks moored under the cranes, or anchored in the stream." Peggy and Douglas Shepperd's "The Story of Port Navas" (1994) provides ample proof of the importance of the village to the granite industry, and includes some fascinating old photographs of granite being loaded or stored here. I can heartily recommend their book to all who want to know more about this delightful and interesting village - and not merely because it is published by Landfall!

Return to the road and turn left up the hill. The painted statues in the porch at Pennance, on the left, are not figureheads from old boats, but were brought here from a Plymouth garden about a century ago. **After about half a mile you reach a crossroads.**

The quay and oysterbeds at Port Navas

❻ Go over the stile opposite. **The footpath cuts across the right-hand corner of the field and then follows the hedge on the right.** The view to the left here is of Polwheveral Creek. **Cross the stile and continue in the same direction - heading towards Constantine church - to the field corner, where there is a stile to the road.**

❼ **Turn right** - or perhaps "keep straight on" is more accurate - **on the road, and at the crossroads turn left, back down towards Polwheveral.**

❽ **Turn right immediately past Polwheveral Cottage and walk up the track that follows the right side of the wooded valley.**

❾ **At the road, turn left.** This is Ponjeravah (pronounced "Ponjerayvah"), where Wheal Vyvyan had one of its two sets of stamps for ore-crushing. You could now continue along the road back into Constantine, but I don't recommend it: it's quite busy and has no pavement. For an attractive alternative that adds about half a mile to the distance, **turn right immediately after crossing the bridge, then left beside a white metal gate by the sign, Low Barn, and go along the path beside the stream. After about half a mile, all of which is quite near the stream, the track bends right. Soon after that, and just before another track comes in from the right, take the narrower path sharp left, crossing the stream.**

As shown on the sketch map, if instead of taking this turning you continued on the main track, you would reach land belonging to Retallack Farm. There, not far from the public footpath but on private land on the other side of the stream, are some fascinating and quite possibly unique remains of a late medieval Cornish tin-processing plant, including the ruins of at least six buildings, variously used as crazing mills, stamping mills and blowing houses - all water-powered, of course. An article about the Retallack site appeared in the journal "Cornish Archaeology" in 1985. If you are interested in seeking permission to view the remains, telephone the farm owner, Mr David Hyde, on 01326-40235.

On the way towards Constantine, ignore side-paths to the left; continue uphill, out of the valley to the houses at Comfort ("crooked way"). The tall chimney on the right is all that remains on surface of Wheal Vyvyan copper mine. **After the steps down, bear right, and then follow the surfaced road back into Constantine.** When you reach the road you will be close to the Queen's Arms; if you continue ahead along Church Square you can return to your car via the churchyard, turning right on the road beyond it.

WALK 10

MAWNAN SMITH, TRENARTH & TREGARNE

About four and a half miles, or three and a half if Mawnan is omitted.

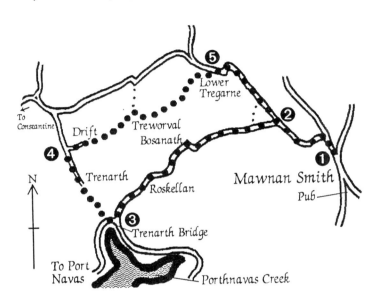

Although you see the Helford only once on this walk, it's one I'd hate to leave out, because it passes through such beautiful and varied countryside. About half a mile of this walk and Walk 9 cover the same ground, in opposite directions. More than half the route is on roads, but very quiet ones, and the mile-or-more down to Trenarth Bridge is outstandingly pretty. Most of the return half of the walk is along farm tracks and footpaths through fields and woodland, passing several interesting and attractive old farms. To me, the great thing about this walk is the strong contrast between the almost cosy wooded valley of the first half and the exhilarating panoramic views of the second. The going is mostly easy, although there are one or two fairly steep climbs on the way back, and if the weather has been wet recently there will be at least one very muddy patch to negotiate on the path between Treworval and Tregarne. It would be easy to avoid that by taking the nearby road instead. About a mile could be knocked off the total distance by omitting the section between

55

Mawnan Smith and Boskensoe: this has to be covered twice, and is comparatively dull walking. The drawback to the shorter alternative is that there are few places where you could park a car except in Mawnan. You might find space at Trenarth Bridge, but please bear in mind that lorries service the factory there. Refreshments can be bought only at Mawnan.

Directions for driving to Mawnan Smith and suggestions for parking there are given for Walk 13.

❶ **Go along the Mabe/Penryn road (Sampys Hill) north out of Mawnan, and take the first turning left, signposted Constantine and Helston.** This soon brings you to Boskensoe Farm.

❷ **Fork left on to a narrow, unsignposted road just beyond Boskensoe.** Very soon you will see, between the roadside trees, the valley sloping away to your right, with lush pastures leading down to woods. One of many attractive old buildings on this route is Bosanath Farm; Bosanath Mill comes later, but is not visible from the road. (Bosanath, by the way, seems to mean "House house"!) At Roskellan (sometimes spelt Roskilling) the road was littered with sweet chestnuts when we passed in October. From here on the road is through woodland, and close by on the right is what looks like an old watermill leat. (There were mills at Tregarne and Bosanath, and it would be surprising if there was not another at or near Trenarth Bridge.) About a hundred yards south of Roskellan there was once a small mine, Wheal Bosanath, which seems to have been active in the 1830s: Hamilton Jenkin mentions a shaft and two adits (drainage shafts); so some of the disturbed ground on both sides of the road could be relics of that. As you approach the river you will see the roofs of I. Knibb & Son's light engineering factory tucked unobtrusively in the valley. Its main business is the finishing of rough castings for appliances such as vacuum cleaners.

❸ **On reaching Trenarth Bridge, at the head of one branch of Porthnavas Creek, turn right immediately: the path up the west side of the valley starts beside a tall granite gatepost on the left of the house (Bridge Cottage).** After a few yards, ignore the wide, level track: keep left, on **the narrower, uphill path. Don't deviate from the main path, and you should soon reach granite steps up to a small metal gate on the edge of the wood. Go through this and continue straight ahead across the field.** The farm to the right now is Trenarth Manor (*). **For 50 yards you have a hedge on your right, and then you join a farm track hedged on both sides;** after the drive to Trenarth this is a surfaced road.

Low tide at Trenarth Bridge

TRENARTH MANOR

The name, meaning "high farm", appears on documents as early as 1260, but the walled garden, courtyard and kitchen area of the house are Elizabethan. The main block was added about 1763; the Georgian wing has an Adam fireplace. The earliest recorded owners were named Trenerth. In the early 16th century the Manor belonged to a family called Crane, but later it came into the possession of the Trefusis family (owners at that time of the nearby Manor of Treviades), who, the present owner believes, eventually lost it in a game of cards. Douglas and Peggy Shepperd give more details of the history of Trenarth in "The Story of Port Navas"; unfortunately, they have not been able to find any evidence to support the story of the card game.

❹ **About 350 yards later, turn right on to the track marked Drift Farm.** (As with "House house", this name means "Farm farm", since "drift" is a form of "tre". Compare Gillan Creek and Pill Creek.) Once you have passed through the farmyard, the view to the right is magnificent, even though the Helford itself lurks unseen; and a little later you can catch a glimpse of St Anthony Lighthouse, at the mouth of the Fal, ahead.

Continue ahead on the lane to Treworval Farm - yet another with a good range of fine, substantial old buildings, several of which have been renovated, presumably as holiday accommodation.

NOTE: If you would rather not brave mud and possibly barbed wire - though the latter was no problem when I last walked here - you could turn left along the main farm drive and right at the road, continuing on that for over half a mile. Ignore the sharp left turning as the road climbs out of the wooded valley. Pick up the directions again at point 5.

To avoid the road (and to enjoy more attractive woodland), bear slightly right, passing Treworval Cottage Two, then go straight on past another cottage and later a modern house. Go through the six-bar metal gate ahead (not the one up on the left) and keep beside the hedge on the left. (Thanks to cattle, this part of the route was extremely muddy when I was last there.) The next metal gate has a yellow waymarker, but in any case the way is pretty obvious, curving very slightly left to where the very ancient-looking path through the trees begins. To get on to it you have to cross a barbed-wire fence by means of a small and rather flimsy wooden stile: care is needed here. Twenty yards later, cross the moss-covered stile over a wall, and go on down to the little granite footbridge beside an old stone building. This was Tregarne Mill, still in operation, so the owners told us, until 1939. A good time to be here is after heavy rains, when the stream rushes down in rapids over the boulders. Continue ahead up the drive of Tregarne House to the road. ("Tregarne" means "farm by/on the rock-pile": tre-carn.)

❺ Turn right. Soon you pass among the buildings of Lower Tregarne Farm - some of them with low roofs in an advanced state of collapse, revealing how the old scantle slates were hung from thin laths. (By December 1994 a few of the buildings had been patched up, and were on offer as "barn conversions".) From here, simply continue along the road past Boskensoe again, turning right for Mawnan Smith at the T-junction.

WALK 11

DURGAN, MAWNAN SMITH, PENPOLL & TREBAH

*Just over three miles; if Helford Passage is included, about half a mile extra.
See page 86 for an even shorter route.*

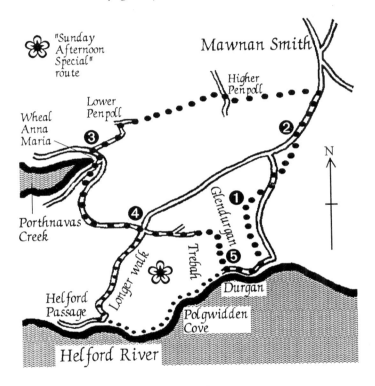

An easy little walk, apart from a couple of fairly steep climbs, through very pleasant countryside. The route includes two of Cornwall's most famous gardens, Trebah and Glendurgan, whose opening dates and times are given in the notes about them included in this walk. The tiny village of Durgan is another special attraction. Waterproof footwear is advisable for the first part of the walk. A total of about half a mile (rather more if you include Helford Passage) is on roads - pretty, rural roads, but they do carry quite a bit of traffic during the summer. The only shops where you could buy provisions on this route are in Mawnan Smith; there are pubs at Mawnan Smith and Helford Passage.

The walk starts at the National Trust car park above Durgan (grid reference: 774277). See Walk 13 for directions to Mawnan Smith. Leave the village on the main road to the south, towards Helford Passage and Port Navas, and take the first turning left, signposted to Durgan. The car park is on the right after a few hundred yards.

❶ **Return to the car park's main entrance and walk back up the road, past the farm** (Bosveal, meaning "home of the Veal family" - which reminds me that Busveal, near St Day, is the home of the Veall family, butchers by trade). Please take care on this narrow road, which can be busy in summer. **As you approach the crossroads sign, take the footpath on the right. After the stile, keep beside the hedge on your right.** Soon you get a pleasant view of the seaward end of the Helford. **After a small, rusty gate and a second stile, bear slightly left, still keeping the hedge on your right. Next comes a wooden stile, and then the path runs alongside gardens. When you come to a granite stile, do not cross it but take the side-path on the left.**

❷ **Turn right at the road, and after about a quarter of a mile you will see a public footpath signposted on the left, opposite a house called Rose Lyon. Take this path, which starts as a very narrow gap between tall wooden garden fences, and soon brings you down to a stile.** (Mud is likely to be a bit of a problem for a while now, but there are helpful, though not always very stable, stepping-stones across the soggiest patches.) **Beyond the stile, the path continues in a fairly straight line across the lower part of the field to a rough stone stile topped by a metal fence, then slightly downhill to a further stile on the left of a farm gate. Now keep by the hedge on your left. Another stile brings you to a farm track at Higher Penpoll. Turn right, passing a couple of houses, and then take the track on the left immediately beyond Barncroft.** (Notice the old granite slab in front of this house, probably from a cider press, and in the back garden some staddle-stones, looking like large granite mushrooms. These were once used to hold up platforms on which hayricks or granaries were built, to protect them from rats and mice. Alternative names are steedstones and sailstones.) **Again the path runs quite straight, keeping beside the hedge on the right, and soon Porthnavas Creek comes into view. Cross the stile over the wall, and then go through the gate on to a track leading to Lower Penpoll (*) farm. Go through the metal gates either side of the farmyard, and follow the concreted (later roughly tarmacked) drive on the left, which soon brings you down to a road beside the creek.**

PENPOLL

The oft-quoted jingle says,

By TRE, POL and PEN
You shall know the Cornishmen.

Not just personal names, but place-names too in Cornwall very often include these elements, and Penpoll - often spelt Penpol in other places - consists of two of them. It can be translated as "end of the pool" or "head of the creek". Few people looking at it now would guess that this was once a mining area. Filled-in shafts and an adit (drainage shaft) big enough to have been used as an air-raid shelter during World War II are at Higher Penpoll. Little is known about that mine, but the one at Lower Penpoll is well documented and was being worked as recently as 1908. Called Wheal Anna Maria after the name of the owner of the land, it had begun producing copper and silver plus a little gold by 1833. The lode (seam) runs north/south under the head of the creek, and two shafts were sunk, one at the entrance to the farm and the other a few yards south of the road bridge. It is still obvious where the second one was - a patch of rough ground with a scattering of rubbish on it. The lode was quite rich, but it seems that all attempts to make good profits from the mine were foiled by flooding problems.

Porthnavas Creek from Lower Penpoll

❸ If the tide is low enough here, you have the chance of a pleasant stroll among the boats along the foreshore. **To continue the walk, go up the road on the left for a few yards, and then take the lane on the right. After about thirty yards, where this curves right, go through the narrow gap on the left (not too painful a squeeze, I hope!) into the field, and then walk uphill, heading just to the left of the house at the top.** The view of Port Navas to the right is not the only breathtaking thing on this part of the walk! At least it provides a welcome excuse, if you feel you need one, for several long pauses as you climb. **Cross the stile and then continue uphill on the road - another narrow one which can be quite busy at times. After Budock Vean Hotel and Cottage comes the turning to Helford Passage.** Tower House, on the corner, was originally the Trebah estate's laundry. The tower was used for water storage for the estate until about 1942.

❹ Here you have a choice to make:
You could walk down the road to Helford Passage (*) (perhaps after visiting Trebah gardens: see below). Good food and drink are available at the attractively situated Ferryboat Inn. **From there, take the coastal footpath, which starts at the east end of the beach. This takes you past Polgwidden Cove (*) to Durgan, where you pick up the directions again at point 5.**

HELFORD PASSAGE
A passenger ferry between here and Helford village has been in operation for many centuries, and as long ago as 1801 the boatmen were already notorious for keeping

travellers waiting while they boozed at what was then called the Passage Inn. "Cornish War and Peace" tells of more recent guests at the Ferryboat, including "Monty" before D-Day. At the western end of Helford Passage is the beach known as the Bar, where traditionally every year people come on Good Friday, armed with buckets and spades, to gather cockles; "trigging" is the local name for it. Unfortunately, such shellfish are particularly vulnerable to the kind of pollution - both agricultural and domestic - to which rivers like the Helford are subjected.

POLGWIDDEN COVE

The name probably means "white pool", or "place with pool and stream". The pillbox, the surfaced road and the fortifications around Trebah's private beach are reminders of fears of enemy invasion, and also of the time when access to the coast was required so that tanks and sections of the Mulberry Harbour could be loaded on to barges for the Normandy landings. The Trebah Garden leaflet refers to it as "Yankee Beach". For more detail, see "Operation Cornwall 1940-1944" by Viv Acton & Derek Carter. The photograph on page 112 is particularly fascinating.

A slightly shorter alternative is to take the footpath to Durgan via Trebah and Glendurgan. For this, continue straight ahead along the drive signposted Public Path and Trebah Farm. Ignore the left turn further on, leading to a picturesque group of old farm buildings. **Soon you reach the entrance to Trebah Gardens (*). Still go straight ahead. When you come to an open field, keep by the hedge on the left. Before long the path bends to the right and descends beside Glendurgan Garden (*),** which can often be entered via a kissing-gate at the bottom, although the official entrance is from the road above the car park. **Soon you enter Durgan village (*).**

TREBAH GARDENS

Trebah Manor (pronounced "Tree-bah", with the stress on the first syllable) was the home of Charles Fox (1797-1878), a prominent member of the influential Falmouth Quaker family whose wealth was derived mainly from their interests in shipping, mining and heavy industry. Several famous gardens owe their existence to the Fox family, and Charles planted this one mainly during the 1850s, although some planting had been done as early as the 1820s. The garden covers 26 acres and is centred on a wooded ravine sloping down to the river. Like most Cornish gardens, it is at its most spectacular in the spring, when the superb collection of azaleas, rhododendrons, camellias, magnolias and pieris are in full colour, but there are also two-and-a-half acres of hydrangeas, many sub-tropical ferns, shrubs and palms, and a recent addition is a large water-garden stocked with Koi carp. The gardens are open to the public from 10.30 a.m. to 5 p.m. all year round (1994 details), and admission to the gardens also includes access to the private beach.

GLENDURGAN

Glendurgan garden is another creation of the Fox family, and the house is still occupied by a branch of it, although the garden was presented to the National Trust in 1962. Much of the note about Trebah applies equally to Glendurgan, which is also a valley garden. One of its special features is a laurel maze, created by Alfred Fox in 1933. Part of the garden known as the Bhutan Valley will be open to the public for the first time in 1995. The National Trust has recently opened a shop at Glendurgan. The garden is open to the public every day except Sunday and Monday between 1st March and 31st October, from 10.30 a.m. to 5.30 p.m. It is also open on Bank Holiday Mondays between those dates, but closed on Good Friday (1994 details).

DURGAN

The name seems to mean "hill, down" (goon) "by the water" (dour). This tiny hamlet, in the care of the National Trust, has retained much of the character of the fishing village it once was. The school was presented to the village in 1876 by the then owner of Bosveal, a Mr Pearce, whose estates included Durgan; until that time the children had had their lessons in the loft of a fish-cellar on the same site. During its days as a school it doubled as a church, and when the pupils deserted it for Mawnan School it became a reading room and library. While the village fishermen were out in their boats at night, usually seeking red mullet, a light was always left on in the reading room to guide them home. An anonymous piece written for the Mawnan Smith W.I. Scrapbook in 1951 tells how the fishermen's wives sold the fish: "The fish was put in wallets or panniers on donkeys and sold to the houses as they went along .... The women also dug for cockles, winkles and limpets, cooked them, and twice a week walked to Falmouth with a bag over each arm. When they had sold their fish, they then brought their household stores, and if they needed coal, brought that home too."

❺ **Turn left past the Old School House and walk up the hill.** On sunny days, I always think the Helford has a Mediterranean holiday postcard look as glimpsed through the Monterey pines at Durgan. A very different picture is painted in *Operation Cornwall*, which tells of tanks containing a mixture of petrol and oil set up in Grebe Woods in 1944 to feed a system of flame throwers on the beach below, for use in the event of a German invasion. *(If you want to go down to the attractive Grebe Beach, take the first path on the right; alternatively, to join the coastal footpath leading to Rosemullion Head, continue up the road almost to where it bends left, and take the path on the right there.)* **To return to the National Trust car park, watch for a short flight of steps up into the wood on the left, about a hundred yards before the left bend in the road. The steps bring you on to a pleasant path which leads direct to the car park; at Bosloe, about half-way up, there are two stiles to cross.**

WALK 12

MAWNAN CHURCH, ROSEMULLION, TOLL POINT & CARWINION

About four and a half miles, or about three miles if Carwinion is omitted. For a very short walk to Toll Point, see page 86.

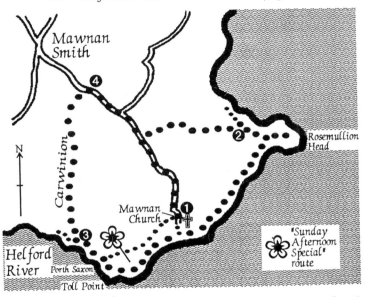

With the possible exception of the section on road - and even that is mostly very pleasant - this walk is a constant delight. For well over half the time you have wonderful sea and river views: few places on the coastal footpath can beat Rosemullion Head as a viewpoint, but many would claim that Toll Point is even better, providing as it does a magnificent panorama of the Helford from Nare Point to Polwheveral Creek. You also have the opportunity to visit an ancient and pretty church, and if you decide to include Carwinion you may wish to explore Carwinion Garden, which is open to the public throughout the year. Alternatively, the walk up the Carwinion valley via the public path is very worthwhile, despite the fact that the only direct route back to Mawnan Church from the top of the valley is nearly a mile along the road. The full walk route is mostly on clear, well-made tracks and paths, and you should not be troubled too much by mud except during very wet spells; there are plenty of stiles to negotiate, but no awkward ones, and you will not have to climb any steep

65

hills. There is no shop or pub along the way, but if you include the Carwinion section you will emerge at the road only about a quarter of a mile from the Red Lion and the shops in Mawnan Smith.

For directions to Mawnan Smith, see Walk 13. To drive to Mawnan Church, take Carwinion Road from the centre of the village: in other words, turn left at the Red Lion if you have approached the village from the north. Where the road bends left at the entrance to the Nansidwell Hotel, turn right. The church is at the end of this road, and there is usually room to park there, although at peak holiday times and during services you may have to find a roadside space further up the road.

❶ The church (*) is worth inspecting, even though the interior has been very thoroughly Victorianised.

MAWNAN CHURCH

For me, the real glory of Mawnan church is its setting. It is not surprising to learn (from the excellent guide on sale in the church) that it was built within an ancient earthwork, because the site, overlooking the river-mouth, is so obviously suitable for a fort. The building itself makes a pretty picture as seen from the churchyard: the tower dates from the 14th century and most of the rest from the 15th. No doubt the 19th century restorers made many changes to the exterior, but if so they are not obtrusive; inside, however, their transformation of the old building and its contents was very thorough indeed. John Betjeman says the church "was so violently restored in 1880 as to be almost new"; according to the church guide, even greater damage was done about fifty years earlier. All this seems regrettable now, but in fairness one should bear in mind the ruinous state into which so many churches had fallen about that time: a report from about 1820 on this one revealed "roofs falling and leaking, seats decaying, windows incapable of opening, and the earth outside the building rising to the windows". The church is obviously lovingly tended nowadays, and the beautiful collection of embroidered kneelers is worth inspection. Much effort and expense have gone into the renovation of the church roof in recent months.

Nothing definite seems to be known about St Mawnan or Maunanus; the church is dedicated also to St Stephen, probably because some bishops were unhappy about shadowy Celtic saints.

Things of interest outside the church include a small ancient cross, originally discovered when the lych-gate was built (1881), and now incorporated in the west wall of the north aisle; the Cornish inscription on the lych-gate, which means, "It is good for me to draw nigh unto God"; and a Holy Well which is described in detail on pages 8-9 of the guide. The well is on private ground, in the garden of The Sanctuary, which is the old rectory - the beautiful house on the left at the S-bend as you walk towards Mawnan Smith. If you would like to see the well, *please contact the owner, Mr J. Simmons, preferably by ringing (0326-250676) some time before you plan to visit.*

When you are ready to start the walk, **go back up the road for about half a mile, and then turn right on to a surfaced lane with a National Trust notice saying "Footpath Only to Rosemullion Head".** (This comes immediately before a house with the rather strange name of "Bo Bod".) Almost at once you have a fine view to the left across Falmouth Bay to Pendennis, St Mawes and St Anthony Lighthouse; later, cranes at Falmouth Docks come into view, and on the skyline far beyond them the white "mountains" created by the china clay industry around St Austell. **Soon you reach Rosemullion Farm, and here a National Trust sign directs you to the left. After the stile, keep on the left side of the hedge ahead** - and now you can also see across the mouth of the Helford to Nare Head.

❷ **On reaching the coastal footpath at the bottom, cross the stile on your right and walk towards Rosemullion Head (*).** I strongly recommend you to take the side path which skirts the headland, because the view from the point is breathtaking: in clear weather it extends from the Manacles (near Porthoustock) southwards, and as far as Dodman Point (south of Mevagissey) to the east.

ROSEMULLION HEAD

It seems only right that so beautiful a place should have a name to match. Of course, it's got nothing to do with roses: ros, as in "Roseland", refers to a promontory. For many years I supposed that "mullion" indicated that there was once a windmill on the headland: it's an ideal spot for one; but Oliver Padel tentatively suggests that the name derives from melhyonen, clover-plant. If you've ever seen Rosemullion when the gorse, the primroses or both are in bloom, you'll be attracted to yet another possible explanation: melyn is Cornish for "yellow".

However, if you're short of time, or if a Cornish mist has descended, **you could cut across the neck of the headland by keeping beside the hedge. Don't go through the farm gate, but continue down towards the river and cross the stile on the right at the bottom.**
The coast path is clear ahead, keeping close to the edge of the low cliff. You cross a footbridge and several more stiles; after the third one a National Trust sign announces Mawnan Glebe (that is, the land attached to the parish church), **and now the path runs through woodland** - a delightful spot on a sunny day, when beyond the dark trunks the sun glints on green leaves, white rocks and blue water. **After climbing a few steps and crossing another stile you are out in the open again and heading across the curved meadow towards Toll Point.** (The name

presumably refers to a cave, since toll is the Cornish word for a hole, as in Mên-an-Tol, the "holed stone" near Madron in West Penwith, and also the Tolvan Stone near Gweek, which is on the route of Walk 8.) I have already, in the introductory note, made it obvious that this is among my favourite places, so I shall resist the temptation to wax lyrical again.

The Helford from near Toll Point

When you are ready to continue walking, **go down the steepish slope on the right to the little stony beach at Porthallack.** (The name probably means "marshy cove", and except during unusually dry spells the ground on the landward side of the wooden boathouse tends to support that interpretation.)

From here you can, if you wish, return direct to Mawnan Church by using the very pretty path up the valley, which keeps just to the right of the stream until you are almost at the top; there you take the track on the right, starting between two granite posts, and cross the stile on the right of the gate near the church.

To extend the walk, continue along the coast after going through the gate behind the boathouse. Soon you come to another stony beach, only a little larger than the first. This one is called Porth Saxon, the Englishmen's cove or harbour - no-one seems to know why. The original Cornish name would have been Porth Zowzon, and despite the anglicised spelling on the maps it is still locally pronounced as Porth Sawsen. Like Polgwidden (Walk 11), Porth Saxon has its souvenir of the threat of German invasion, in the form of a concrete "pill-box". Cross to the far side of the beach.

❸ **Turn right through a gate on to the inland path signed Carwinion Valley. The path is clear and well-walked, keeping just to the left of the** stream most of the way up the valley: a very attractive woodland walk. After a kissing-gate you enter an open field, but almost at once a second kissing-gate brings you back among the trees. At the small gate to Carwinion Garden (*) the public footpath keeps to the left, and there are a couple of stiles. Keep to the main track as it bears right past farm buildings, until eventually it emerges at a road beside the main entrance to Carwinion.

CARWINION GARDEN

Like so many of the famous gardens in this area, Carwinion occupies a valley. In addition to the spring-flowering shrubs typical of most Cornish gardens, Carwinion has an important collection of about a hundred species of bamboo. The garden is open every day throughout the year from 10 till 5.30, admission £1, under-12s free (1994 details). The name "Carwinion" probably indicates that there was once an ancient fort, round or camp nearby - and indeed the O.S. maps indicate one just a few hundred yards to the west.

❹ If you are in need of refreshments, you may be able to get a cream tea at Carwinion; otherwise, it's a walk of about a quarter of a mile to the left to the Red Lion and shops. **Turn right to return to the church, keeping right at the sign to the Nansidwell hotel and restaurant; about a mile of road-walking** through an area which has been quite heavily developed during the past few decades for holiday homes, retirement bungalows and country residences for commuters to places like Truro and Falmouth - but there are attractive older buildings too: cottages, mansions and farms.

WALK 13
MAWNAN SMITH & MAENPORTH

Just over three miles.

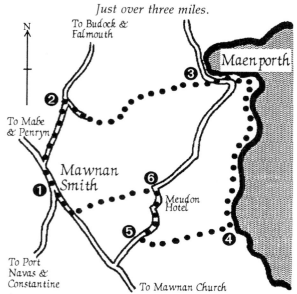

Based on the quite large, beautifully situated village of Mawnan Smith, this walk takes you down one attractive, wooded valley and later up a second one; between the two is a beautiful short section of the coastal footpath. Maenporth, a little less than half way along the route, offers safe bathing and probably the best beach in the area; it has a pub where good food is served (and by that I do not intend to cast any aspersions on the drink!), and also during the season a beach café and toilets. A smaller beach and another opportunity for bathing comes near the end of the coastal section. Shops and another good pub can be found at the centre of Mawnan Smith. There is about half a mile of road walking in the village, and about a quarter of a mile along a country road which tends to carry quite a lot of traffic during the summer. Waterproof footwear would be advisable.

To drive to Mawnan Smith (*) from Falmouth, take the new Penryn bypass road. Mawnan Smith is signposted from the first (Hillhead) roundabout. After about two miles on the B3291 turn left, again where signposted to Mawnan Smith. To drive from Helston, turn off the A394 Penryn / Falmouth / Truro road on to the new bypass road towards Falmouth at the Kernick roundabout, continue on that till you reach the Hillhead roundabout, and proceed as above. Routes via Gweek and / or Constantine may be more direct but involve many narrow, twisting roads and *require an observant map reader. There is no public car park in Mawnan Smith, but roadside parking should be available near the centre of the village - perhaps in the layby near the Post Office/general store. If you decide to patronise the Red Lion you may be able to leave your car there.*

MAWNAN SMITH

John Betjeman calls it "an old village", and this is confirmed by some surviving old buildings, including the thatched, cob-walled pub, dating back to the 15th century, and also by the name, which refers to a blacksmith's shop. (Compare "Barkla Shop", near St Agnes.) Other names within the village, such as Carwinion and Carlidnack, suggest habitation in very early times, and the round mentioned in section 2 confirms this. Since the parish church is so distant, a second church or chapel of ease, St Michael's, was built within the village in 1876. Mawnan Smith has grown rapidly during the past century, and no-one who looks at its setting will need to be told why. The massive preparations for D-Day required the widening of the road through the village: see "Operation Cornwall", page 111. The book also includes a well-known photograph of US troops passing the Red Lion in 1944.

❶ From the Red Lion, walk back a few yards to the Post Office and take the right turning, Carlidnack Road.

❷ After about half a mile, turn right on to Carlidnack Lane. A little way along, notice on the left the bungalow named "The Round Field"; the lane beside this leads to the remains of an ancient round or fort. For details see *Cornish Archaeology*, issue 15 (1976). The first syllable of "Carlidnack" may derive from Cornish *ker*, a round or fort; alternatively, the name may refer to holly *(kelin)*. **At the derestriction sign, where the road turns left, bear right, passing a blue notice, "Private - No Cars". Ignore the public footpath to Meudon on the right, but when you come to two farm gates bear right and follow the public footpath sign to Maenporth. Soon another footpath sign directs you to the right, over a footbridge, across a stile and then a second footbridge into woodland. After the next stile the path continues more-or-less straight ahead along the left edge of a field, with to your left the woodland and views of Maenporth (*) beach and the sea beyond. Continue down past a metal gate to a wooden stile beside a public footpath sign; cross the stile and turn right to reach the road.**

MAENPORTH

The name (pronounced Main-porth) means "stone cove" or "rocky cove", but in fact there is a lot more fine sand on Maenporth beach than on others nearby. Holiday apartments have now been built on the hill overlooking the beach; the cove was dominated by the Crag Hotel until it was destroyed by fire in 1982. There is evidence that during the last Ice Age, forest covered not only the valley above but also the area that now forms the beach; as the temperatures rose the lower trees were submerged. Occasionally storms shift the sand enough to reveal remains of the forest, and in the County Museum in Truro is a report dated 1895 which tells how in that year a layer of softened wood and mould several feet deep was revealed; in it were found fircones, a deer antler and the fossilised jawbone of an early species of horse.

❸ Unless you want to use the beach and its facilities, cross the road and turn right on the coastal footpath, soon passing the shed belonging to the Falmouth Surf Life Saving Club. Keep to the landward side of the mesh fencing later: the cliff here is very unstable. Look back for a good view of Maenporth and the rusting hulk of the Ben Asdale (*) on the rocks on the far side of the cove.

THE "BEN ASDALE"

A search of local libraries and second-hand bookshops may yield a copy of a booklet by Frank Pearce called "Mayday! Mayday! Mayday!" It gives a vivid account of the air-sea rescue work done by the helicopter crews from RNAS Culdrose, near Helston. My only regret about the book is that it was written just a few months too soon to report one of the most dramatic and courageous rescues carried out by the Culdrose airmen. One stormy night in December 1978 - New Year's Eve, in fact - the Aberdeen trawler "Ben Asdale" was driven on to the rocks at Maenporth. Coastguards tried to use a breeches buoy to save the crew, but the equipment was damaged when the ship rolled. Would-be rescuers watched helplessly as several men were swept overboard by a huge wave. Despite the high winds, a helicopter pilot managed to hover within inches of a cliff-edge lit up only very faintly by flares being fired from a lifeboat; a coastguard armed with a radio gave guidance. Eight of the trawler's crew were winched aboard and three others were found alive in the sea or on the rocks. The battered hull of the ship remains as a reminder of that memorable night.

Soon the view is restricted by hedges on both sides as the path runs beside gardens, but when you emerge into the open you are rewarded with a fine view of Rosemullion Head. (See the note in Walk 12.) In spring there is a wonderful show of primroses on a bank here. After a few steps up, there are more high hedges, but with glimpses of the sea, and at the top of the next slope it's worth looking back for the superb view to St Anthony Lighthouse by Zone Point. **Beyond the next stile, the path follows the left edge of a field. The stile following that is overgrown, so you have to duck under a fence. Now the path descends towards a small beach and** the grounds of the Meudon Hotel. Continue along the coast path over two more stiles.

4 **When you come to a wooden post with acorn signs and yellow Waymark arrows, turn right up the valley path which runs close by a stream on the left.** *(Alternatively, of course, for a longer walk you could continue along the coast towards Rosemullion, joining the route of Walk 12 at point 2; then from Porthallack you could visit Mawnan church, returning to the coast after that and walking back to Mawnan Smith via the Carwinion valley as directed.)* **At a farm gate the path continues a little to the right. Later you go through a wooden gate, and a surfaced drive brings you to a road.**

5 **Turn right, and walk facing the oncoming traffic, which can be quite speedy. Continue past Chenhalls** (pronounced *Sh'nalls* and meaning either "house on the moor" or "house on the cliff"), **Firs Lodge and the Meudon Hotel.**

6 **At the sharp right corner, cross to the footpath signposted to Mawnan Smith, starting at a high stone stile. Keep by the hedge on the right, and after a few yards cross another stile. Now for two fields the hedge is on your left; then another stile, and you are on the left of the hedge again. One final stile brings you to the road on the edge of Mawnan Smith. Turn right, and you are soon back at the Red Lion.**

Near Rosemullion: looking back towards Falmouth

WALK 14

SWANPOOL, PENJERRICK & MAENPORTH

About four miles.

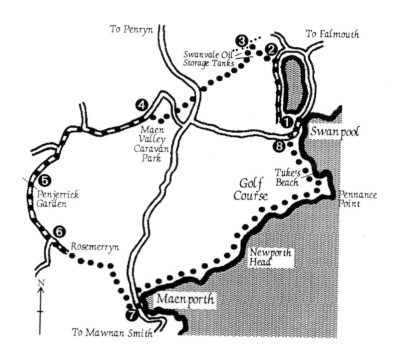

Walk 13 wasn't exactly "around the Helford", I admit, and this one is even further away; I hope you will look on them and No. 15 as a bonus. (I did consider *From Helford to Fal* as a title, but it's a clumsy mouthful!) Penjerrick garden is far too good to leave out, and so is the coastal walk between Maenporth and Swanpool; the inland section is through pretty countryside, including two wooded valleys. This is quite an easy walk, though there is a longish uphill stretch approaching Penjerrick. About a mile is on quiet country roads. There are two popular beaches en route; one (Maenporth) has a pub, and both have light refreshments and public toilets in season. Penjerrick garden is open to the public on Wednesday and Sunday afternoons (1.30 - 4.30) from March to September.

Swanpool (*) beach is on the southern edge of Falmouth and has a large car park.

SWANPOOL

The small lake was kept by its former owners, the Killigrews, for swan breeding. Swanpool is like a miniature version of Loe Pool, a freshwater lake near Porthleven which is cut off from the sea by a bar of sand and shingle. At Loe Bar a pipeline has been built to the sea to prevent flooding; so also here a small tunnel was constructed by "the industry of one poor man and his son", to quote "The Selector" of 1826, in order to keep the road safe from floods. In fact the original road, closer to the sea than now, was destroyed by easterly gales in 1917: hence all the granite blocks on the beach.

A lead-and-silver mine was started at Swanpool early in the 18th century, and during the 1850s it had a workforce of over a hundred, had sunk three shafts and was employing a 40-inch beam engine. (The measurement refers to the diameter of the cylinder.) At about this time an enormously long flue to collect arsenic deposits was built from the smelting furnace on the south side of the cove to Pennance Point, where two chimneys were erected; the headland is still known locally as "The Stack". The mine itself closed down soon after, but for several years from 1875 arsenic was refined in the old smelting house, and it used to be regarded as dangerous to eat blackberries picked nearby. Four fascinating photographs showing these features, together with detailed historical explanations, are to be found in Peter Gilson's "Falmouth in Old Photographs". What is now the car park and the "Skid Kids" self-drive motorbike circuit was still marshland till the latter part of World War II, when US army engineers covered it with material from Swanpool Mine's burrows (waste tips) to create an area for practising fire-fighting techniques.

Swan Pool Mine (based on an old engraving)

❶ From the back of the car park, take the road that runs along the western edge of the pool. The pool itself - a wildlife habitat classified as one of the eleven most important saline lagoons in the country - is, in fact, hidden from this road by trees and marsh plants for the first hundred yards or so. This 2-acre area of wet woodland is a nature reserve maintained by the Cornwall Wildlife Trust and the Gyllyngvase Residents' Association.

❷ As you approach the end of the pool, turn left and take the tarmacked footpath that runs beside the stream.

❸ At the wider lane turn left and immediately left again, under a footbridge, on to an uphill path which takes you among the oil-storage tanks of Swanvale (*).

SWANVALE OIL-STORAGE TANKS

They are less of an eyesore than they may sound, being carefully buried and landscaped, for security as well as environmental reasons. Despite such precautions, a German U-Boat Captain's map which came to light after the war clearly showed their position. "Mental pictures remain," writes Bob Dunstan in his "Book of Falmouth and Penryn", "of vast clouds of black smoke from burning subterranean oil tanks near Swanvale, breached by a bomb, when a local bulldozer driver heroically damped down the flames with earth, at great risk to himself." One wonders whether such "mental pictures" ever occur to owners of the many houses since built close by! The successful attack took place just after midnight on 30 May 1944, destroying fuel vital for the imminent Normandy landings. A dramatic account of what happened, and an equally dramatic on-the-spot photograph, are in "Operation Cornwall 1940-1945" by Viv Acton and Derek Carter. They also mention that the Cornish Auxiliary Unit (part of the "Secret Army" of trained resistance fighters) had been assigned two principal missions in the event of a German invasion: to blow up the Royal Albert Bridge over the Tamar, and to set fire to the storage tanks at Swanvale.

Continue through the group of houses. At the road, the path goes on opposite, and at the next road cross the stile opposite. The path here is rather narrow for the first few yards and tends to be somewhat overgrown with nettles and brambles, but then continues clear along the curving right-hand edge of a field. The large house you will see to the right is Roscarrack (possibly "moor rock", though early versions of the name suggest that "carrack" is actually a corruption of a personal name, "Cadok"). **At a gap in the barbed-wire fence, steps lead down to another road, where you will again find the path continues nearly opposite.** This section is particularly pretty, with a valley view and a glimpse of Budock Water village to the right. Finally the path runs beside a caravan park.

❹ At the next road (by the entrance to Maen Valley Park and a post box marked "Lower Crill"), turn left - another uphill stretch. Keep left at the next road junction, and soon on your right is the entrance to Penjerrick (*). The 15-acre garden is famous for its rhododendrons, but also has many other shrubs and fine specimen trees in a beautiful setting looking down to the sea. Below the footbridge is a big pond area surrounded by almost wild vegetation.

PENJERRICK

The Penjerrick estate came into the possession of the Fox family (already mentioned in the note on Trebah, Walk 11) early in the 19th century. From 1818 it was the summer residence of Robert Were Fox (1789-1877). Robert was an inventor, best known for the Fox Deflector Dipping Needle, used in early polar expeditions. He and his daughters, Anna Maria and Caroline (founders of the Royal Cornwall Polytechnic Society, based in Falmouth, in 1833), entertained such celebrities as Wordsworth, Coleridge, Carlyle, Tennyson and Holman Hunt.

❺ When you are ready to go on, continue along the road in the same direction. Soon you will pass under the wooden bridge which leads from the upper to the lower sections of the garden.

❻ Where the road bends sharply right, go straight on through the gateway signposted Rosemerryn (*) Farm. At the big gates leading to the imposing Georgian-style house go left, following the blue waymark arrow and the small sign "Footpath to Maenporth".

ROSEMERRYN

"Rosmeryn" or "Rosmerin" (meaning "Merin's heath") is mentioned in documents dating back to the early 13th century, and a mansion there was occupied by John Rosmaren in 1414. By the middle of the 18th century the mansion was falling into ruin, and the present house presumably replaced it soon after that. By 1841 Rosemerryn, like so many other properties in this district, had come into the possession of the Fox family - in this case, Charles Fox, owner of Trebah. His Rosemerryn estate included a "Summer House" and "Pleasure Grounds" above Maenporth beach - later the site of the Crag Hotel.

At the rough lane, turn right, then left where there is another small and rather faded Maenporth sign. This path, its pleasant valley views only slightly marred by the caravan site, leads straight down to the beach, passing the Seahorse Inn just before the road. (Notes on Maenporth and the *Ben Asdale* are included under Walk 13.)

❼ **The coast path back to Swanpool leaves the north side of the beach just behind the refreshments building;** here also you will find the toilets. The path is well-trodden and presents no complications. When you reach the point where you are roughly opposite the headland on the far side of the cove, a small side path running by the cliff-edge around an open, grassy field affords a good close-up view of the rusted remains of the *Ben Asdale*. A little further on, at Newporth Head, there is a slipway dating from about 1830, the purpose of which no-one now seems to know. From roughly there onwards, the path runs beside the Falmouth golf course. Unless you are blessed with a Cornish mist, from the earlier section of this coastal stretch you will have fine views south to Rosemullion Head and The Manacles, and later north to Falmouth and Pendennis, and St Anthony lighthouse on the far side of the harbour mouth. After rounding Pennance ("head of the valley") Point, when you emerge from the woodland you will see on your right the remains of the old smelting works which became an arsenic refinery; here and there, parts of the long arsenic flue have also survived. The small cove nearby became known as Tuke's Beach because it was frequently used by the "Newlyn School" painter Henry Scott Tuke (1858-1929), who lived for almost the last forty-five years of his life at what had once been the Swanpool Mine manager's house, close by. At such secluded places as this cove he could pursue his special interest in painting nudes outdoors without causing public outrage. The house was demolished many years ago, but it is still possible to locate its foundations, and the steps down to the beach remain.

❽ **At the road, turn right down the hill for Swanpool.**

WALK 15

BUDOCK, PENJERRICK & ROSEMERRYN
WITH A POSSIBLE EXTENSION TO PENWARNE

A little under four miles. The extension would add about another mile.

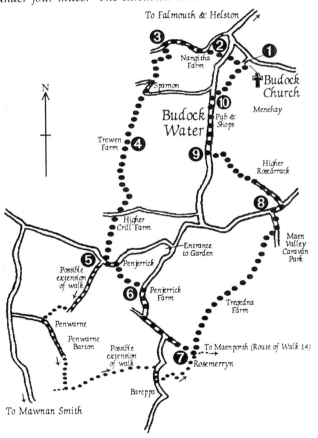

No wonder there are so many fine, expensive-looking houses, old and new, on this route: the countryside is lush-looking, pretty and peaceful; the climate favours "sub-tropical" garden plants, especially in the sheltered valleys; and above all, the views to the east and south are magnificent, taking in Falmouth Harbour and the coast from Zone Point (and there is even a glimpse of Nare Head, Veryan) to the Manacles. The district is rich in paths and bridleways, many of them carefully waymarked, liberally supplied with venerable-looking but sturdy and well maintained granite stiles. Most of the farm tracks and some of the field paths were extremely muddy in January 1995, but this was after a very wet spell. Budock Water has two general stores and a pleasant pub, the Trelowarren Arms.

To drive to Budock from Falmouth, take the new Penryn bypass road and turn left at the first (Hillhead) roundabout. Follow the signs to Budock Water, turning right about half a mile beyond the roundabout, just after you have passed the Falmouth Town football ground (Bickland Park). After almost another half mile, turn left along a narrow side road, which soon brings you to Budock church. Turn right as you reach the slate-hung Vestry Room. The church car park is locked except during services, but there is room for a few cars to park on the churchyard side of the road (left) just beyond the Vestry Room. Please do not park on the other side, beside the Eglos (Cornish for "church") Farm building. To drive here from Helston, take the A394 road towards Truro and Falmouth; turn right towards Falmouth on the new Penryn bypass road at the Treliever roundabout; continue ahead at the Kernick roundabout; and turn right at the Hillhead roundabout. Now continue as above.

BUDOCK PARISH AND CHURCH

The ancient parish of Budock - most of which is visible from the magnificently sited church - was very large, covering part of Penryn including Glasney College (see "A Second View from Carn Marth", page 54), plus the whole of what is now Falmouth. The latter was first separated from the mother parish in 1661 (municipal parish) and 1664 (church parish), and as the town grew so it took over more of Budock parish in the 19th and 20th centuries. The name Budock is that of the church's patron saint, according to legend the son of a Breton princess; she is said to have given birth to him while floating in a barrel towards Ireland, having been falsely accused of adultery. St Budoc is honoured in Brittany and also in the Plymouth area (St Budeaux) and Pembrokeshire (St Botolphs). It appears that, following his education at a monastery in Ireland, he set up a religious foundation south of the present church at Menehay (Cornish, "meneghy", "sanctuary"). Another tradition says that after his death the Saint's right hand was embalmed so that he could offer blessing and absolution for ever; the hand is represented in the church porch, and also appears on the carved staves used by the churchwardens. The earliest known rector of Budock whose incumbency can be dated was here in 1207, and the oldest parts of the church building date from about then; much of it, however, was added in the 15th century, that great period for enlarging churches. In this case the work was probably financed mainly by the Killigrew family of Arwenack; an important memorial brass set into the chancel floor is that of Sir John Killigrew, the first Governor of Pendennis Castle. Another feature inside to note is the Chancel Screen (c. 1500), almost certainly a gift of the Killigrews. It was badly damaged during the Civil War, but many of the original painted panels have survived. Budock is unusual among Cornish churches in still having its old box pews, installed at the end of the 18th century. The slate-hung Vestry Room on the north side of the churchyard was erected in the 1840s, retaining in its structure parts of an old stable and coach house. The Vestry meetings carried out all local administration under the Justices of the Peace; previously the Budock Vestry had met mostly at inns or private houses.

Much of the information in this note and elsewhere in Walks 14 and 15 has been taken from the local Parish History Group's excellent "St Budock - A Short Study of an Ancient Parish", published in two volumes (1974 and 1993). The earlier book is probably obtainable now only secondhand or through libraries, but the later one is still in bookshops and would make a good companion - for example when exploring the churchyard, or if you want to know something of the history of the homes and farms in the parish.

A glimpse of Falmouth Harbour from Budock churchyard

❶ Walk on from the suggested parking place, past the church, and cross the pair of stiles (one granite, one wooden) beside the house named "Barnfield" - at least, it was called that in 1995. Keep beside the wooden fence, following it around the corner to the right. At the end of the fence continue ahead to another stone stile. This brings you to a road.

❷ Cross the stile opposite. The path now runs between hedges, with a small estate of bungalows on the left. After another stile a long coastal view to the left opens up. At Nangitha the path becomes a farm lane.

❸ Not far beyond the farm, turn left at a stone stile - a wooden post with three yellow arrows painted on it marks the spot. (If you are following this route on the "Pathfinder" OS map, you will notice that this path seems to have been moved a little further east than the map shows.) Now walk around the edge of the field with the hedge on your left (more excellent sea and harbour views from here), till you reach farm buildings. Here cross the stone stile on the left, then go a few feet to your right, and turn left on the tarmacked drive. This soon takes you past Sparnon (Cornish, "thorn trees") house, with its panoramic view and its lovely garden sloping down. Where the drive turns sharp left, cross the granite stile ahead. Keep beside the hedge on your right at first. Soon you join a pretty path through woodland; in winter the sound of a stream down to the left filled the air. Ignore the side path to the right as the path starts to descend to the stream, and also the one to the left immediately after crossing the footbridge; keep right at the next junction, and walk up through the last of the wood to a few stone steps up to a Public Footpath sign at the edge of an open field. Continue ahead, still uphill, to a stile at the field corner, and then straight on along a wide track to Trewen (Cornish, "white farmstead"). Trewen (said with the stress on the second syllable) was already one of the largest farms in Budock parish in 1840, and remains so, having absorbed part of what was Sparnon Farm land. The Rev. John Rham in his chapter on Budock church (see the note on Budock Parish and Church) suggests that the names of Sparnon and Trewen may both refer to the blackthorn whose white blossom used to cover even more of their land in spring than it does today.

❹ As you reach the farm buildings, cross the stile on the right (clearly indicated by a sign painted on a water-tank), keep beside the buildings, crossing another stile, and at the end of the last barn go diagonally left to another stile at the field corner. Having crossed that, walk with the hedge on your left and cross yet another stile beside a waymark post. You are now (I hope!) at Higher Crill (Cornish, *ker-kel*, "camp of the shelter"). Turn right on the road, and immediately beyond the last house go left through a wooden farm gate with yellow waymark arrow attached.

The path now runs across the middle of the large field (formerly three smaller ones), giving more good views to the left, including much of Falmouth and a glimpse of Nare Head in the far distance. **It brings you to a stile to the left of a metal farm gate.**

❺ *Here, for an attractive extension of the walk, avoiding some road walking, continue ahead, crossing the road and going through the gate marked Penwarne opposite.*

Please note, however, that unless the weather has been unusually dry you will probably need wellies.

The Penwarne ("top of the alder-grove") drive, a public bridleway, makes delightful walking, surrounded as it is by woodland recently planted with rhododendrons, azaleas and camellias, and with the - by now customary - sea views, this time mainly over Maenporth. As you near the house, you are directed over a stile on the right into a field usually churned up by cattle; then keep near the hedge on your left. After the gate, turn left on the lane, past the house. Where the lane curves left to Penwarne Barton (farm), continue ahead on the farm track. (This is where you'll really be glad of those boots. Perhaps the alternative explanation of "Penwarne", "top of the alder-swamp", is right after all!) There are several gates to negotiate, plus one particularly sticky patch where cattle come to feed. Go right down to the end of this track, cross the two stiles (stone and wooden ones on either side of a hedge) and turn left. Keep to the left side of the field. More good views ahead here. The village to the right is Mawnan Smith. After another stile and three gates, turn right on the road. About 150 yards later, turn left at the footpath sign and stile.

(But first you might like to go a little further along the road to look at Bareppa, a pretty group of farm buildings, cottages and grander houses. The first house's name, "The Kidley-Wink", means it was once a beer-house. The name is said to allude to the fact that you could get stronger liquor from the "kiddle" or kettle if you gave a wink. The attractive Bareppa House has an old cider-press millstone on show. "Bareppa" is said locally as "Breppa", and derives from the French, "beau repair", "beautiful retreat", or possibly "good lodging". The latter meaning is usually suggested for the village of Barripper, south of Camborne, where pilgrims en route for St Michael's Mount are said to have lodged. See "A View from Carn Brea", Walk 7.)

After the next stile, with footbridges over little streams on both sides, go a few paces right, then walk uphill with the hedge on your right. A few steps up bring you to a gravelled path; turn left on that, past the greenhouses at Rosemerryn. After the gate continue ahead past the gates of the house, following the yellow arrow. Now pick up the directions at point 7, line 2.

For the main route shown on my sketch map, however, **turn left on the road, and where that bends left take the Public Bridleway signposted to the right - not the driveway straight ahead, which leads to Penjerrick**

house. (*But if the garden happens to be open and you want to visit it, continue down the road for a further quarter-mile-or-so; the entrance is on the right at the T-junction. To continue the walk from there, follow the road to the right, soon passing under the footbridge, as described in Walk 14, Section 5, and then pick up the directions at the latter part of Section 6 below. For a note on Penjerrick, see Walk 14.*) **The bridleway skirts Penjerrick grounds; it winds downhill, and after a gate becomes a tarmacked drive leading to Penjerrick Vean.**

❻ At the road (notice the pretty wooden Quaker Cottage at Penjerrick Farm opposite, dated 1862)**, turn right, and walk along the road for rather less than half a mile.** The village seen to the right is Mawnan Smith. **Where the road bends right continue ahead along the drive to Rosemerryn.** (See the note on this in Walk 14.)

❼ As you approach the gates to Rosemerryn house turn left, following the yellow waymark arrow. Beyond the metal farm gate a muddy tractor track runs downhill. At another yellow arrow, steps lead down to a very boggy area in a small copse, which would be impassable but for the wooden walkway that spans most of it. Care is needed as you use that, because it tends to be slippery. **Steps lead up on the far side. Keep straight on to a waymark post beside the rough track leading to Tregedna Farm buildings. Continue straight ahead, uphill, still following the yellow arrows. At the next waymark post, where there is a stile, go straight on, ignoring another path going to the left; follow the grassy tractor-track as far as another stile, then walk by the hedge on your right. After the next stile the path runs among trees, with the Maen Valley Caravan Park down on the right. Continue along the right-hand edge of a field, cross a wooden stile and turn left along a lane.**

❽ At the road turn right, then after about a couple of hundred yards take the wide track on the left, marked with a blue wooden arrow. Soon you pass Ponds Cottage. ("Some cottage!" was my wife's comment. The tranquillity of its setting was rudely shattered for a while in World War II when a bomb falling nearby removed the house's roof, windows and hanging slates.) **Ignore the signed path on the right just past that, and keep on along the main track to the left of the entrance drive to Roscarrack Vean. The attractive path runs near the bottom of a shallow valley, then, after a few steps up to a small kissing gate, it goes slightly uphill, through a little furze patch, and brings you to another granite stile. From there it goes along the side of the valley overlooked by Budock church. Just before the first bungalow there are a few steps up, with a small gate, and a short lane (Trelil Lane) takes you to the road.**

❾ Turn right, passing through Budock Water (*) village, where a few traditional Cornish cottages still lurk among the council houses and modern bungalow developments. Trelowarren Terrace, which includes the pub, dates from before 1841, and was originally the property of Sir Richard Vyvyan of Trelowarren - see Walk 6.

BUDOCK WATER

The name probably refers to the stream flowing under the road near the former Methodist Chapel and then down the valley just east of the village, to reach the sea at Maenporth. The original hamlet has now been swamped, like Mawnan Smith, with modern homes for retirement or for families whose breadwinners work in Falmouth or other nearby towns. Most local employment is in or related to agriculture, although the farms need far less labour than they once did, and several have adapted some of their buildings to providing tourist accommodation or homes for the elderly.

⑩ When you reach Budock Methodist Chapel, recently converted into a restaurant called King Arthur's Meadery, **you could take the signed footpath on the right, which leads up to the church. It is steep and rough, though, and a gentler though longer alternative is to keep to the road and take the path you used at the start, or the road on the right beyond that.**

SUNDAY AFTERNOON SPECIALS

A few very short circular walks

FLUSHING AND GILLAN *Under 1½ miles.*
You should be able to park by the road near the Gillan Garage, or at the Tregildry Hotel if you intend to patronise it. Follow direction 5 and most of 6 in Walk 1.

ST ANTHONY AND DENNIS HEAD *Under a mile.* *Dogs not allowed.*
Park at St Anthony church: the car park is signposted on the left before the church. Walk to the east end of the church and join the path at the Bosahan Estate notice. At the acorn sign turn left, and at the second acorn sign turn right to circle Dennis Head as described in Walk 2, point 4.

HELFORD, KESTLE, FRENCHMAN'S CREEK *2-2½ miles.*
Start Walk 3 as described, taking the first side-path as mentioned near the end of point 1. After two stiles, go along the right side of the field, then through Kestle farmyard to the road. Go left a little and follow the footpath opposite to "Frenchman's Pill". At the creek turn right, following the directions again from the later part of point 4 to the end.

CONSTANTINE AND POLWHEVERAL *About 2 miles.*
Follow the directions for Walk 9, points 1 and 2, but turn left just before Polwheveral Cottage, returning to Constantine as per points 8 and 9.

TREBAH, DURGAN, HELFORD PASSAGE *About 1½ miles.*
Park on the left at the top of the road down to Helford Passage. Now follow the directions given for the second part of point 4 in Walk 11. At Durgan turn right; follow the coast path to Helford Passage and take the road back from there to your car.

MAWNAN CHURCH AND TOLL POINT *Less than a mile.*
Park at the church as directed for Walk 12, and take the path from the churchyard to the coastal footpath at Mawnan Glebe. Turn right, and proceed as described in the middle part of point 2, returning up the valley path from Porthallack.

FOOTNOTE 1 The walk to Tremayne Quay and back from the nearest road would also be ideal, but there is very limited parking by the road - and the route isn't circular. (See Walk 5, points 5 and 6.)

FOOTNOTE 2 Walk 4 could have qualified for this page!

FURTHER READING

The books whose titles I have starred are, to the best of my knowledge, currently out of print, but should be available through libraries.

Acton, Viv & Carter, Derek: *Cornish War and Peace; The Road to Victory - and Beyond* (Landfall, 1995) (almost ready for the printers when this edition was being prepared)

Acton, Viv & Carter, Derek: *Operation Cornwall 1940-1944 - The Fal, the Helford and D-Day* (Landfall, 1994)

Budock Parish History Group: *St Budock - A Short Study of an Ancient Parish* Volume I, 1974 *; Volume II, 1993

Chesher, V.M & F.J.: *The Cornishman's House* * (D.Bradford Barton, 1968)

Coate, Mary: *Cornwall in the Great Civil War and Interregnum, 1642-1660* * (D.Bradford Barton, 1963)

Dunstan, Bob: *The Book of Falmouth & Penryn* (Barracuda, 1975)

Foot, Sarah: *Rivers of Cornwall* (Bossiney Books, 1984)

Gilson, Peter: *Falmouth in Old Photographs* (Alan Sutton, 1990)

Henderson, Charles: *A History of the Parish of Constantine in Cornwall* * (King's Stone Press for the R.I.C., 1937)

Jenkin, A.K.Hamilton: *Mines & Miners of Cornwall*, Vol. 13* (Truro Bookshop, 1967)

Le Messurier, Brian: *The Helford River* (National Trust "Coast of Cornwall" leaflet No. 16, 1989)

Luck, Liz: *South Cornish Harbours* (A. & C.Black, 1988)

Newton, Jill: *Bygone Helston & the Lizard* (Phillimore, 1987)

Newton, Jill: *Helford River* * (Treleague / Century Litho, n.d.)

Newton, Jill: *The Lizard* * (Bossiney Books, 1978)

Oates, A.S.: *Around Helston in the Old Days* (1951; facsimile edition by Dyllansow Truran, 1983)

Padel, O.J.: *Cornish Place-Name Elements* (English Place-Name Society, 1985)

Padel, O.J.: *A Popular Dictionary of Cornish Place-Names* (Alison Hodge, 1988)

Shepperd, Peggy & Douglas: *The Story of Port Navas* (Landfall, 1994)

Vyvyan, C.C.: *The Helford River* (Peter Owen, 1956; reprinted by Dyllansow Truran 1986)

Vyvyan, C.C.: *The Old Place* * (Museum Press, 1952)

Witherwick, G.T.: *"Fangs", The Memoirs of a Gardening Dentist* (privately published, 1993; available from Landfall Publications and Victoria Gallery, Cross Street, Camborne)

Witherwick, G.T.: *In A Cornish Valley - A Nature Diary* * (privately published, 1983)

LANDFALL BOOKS

BELOW ARE DETAILS OF THE BOOKS MOST CLOSELY RELATED TO THE HELFORD - FALMOUTH AREA. FOR INFORMATION ABOUT OTHER LANDFALL BOOKS, CONTACT THE ADDRESS BELOW.

THE STORY OF
PORT NAVAS
by Peggy & Douglas Shepperd
£3.99

A well-documented history of this delightful Helford village which has such strong links with granite quarrying, shipping and oyster farming. Generously illustrated with old photographs, sketches and maps.

AROUND THE FAL

Low tide at Coombe

by Bob Acton £2.95
Ten beautiful walks around the Fal estuary. Historical notes, maps & sketches.

A SECOND VIEW
FROM CARN MARTH

Pill Creek, Feock

by Bob Acton £4.95
Fourteen round walks around Truro, Falmouth and Redruth. Historical notes, maps, sketches and full-colour photographs.
This book includes the Mabe and Stithians areas, the fascinating walk from Devoran to Feock, the beautiful and historic Kennall Vale, and the sites of the great Gwennap copper mines.

OPERATION CORNWALL 1940-1944
The Fal, the Helford & D-Day
by Viv Acton & Derek Carter

Published to coincide with the 50th anniversary of D-Day, this fully illustrated book reveals the strategic importance - often overlooked in other studies - of this part of Cornwall.
£5.99

A sequel to OPERATION CORNWALL is in preparation for publication early in 1995. See page 87.

The most recent Landfall book
EXPLORING
CORNISH MINES
by Kenneth Brown & Bob Acton £5.50
Guided tours of six important mine sites, including two within easy reach of the Helford:
The Basset Mines and Dolcoath.
Also Botallack to Boswedden -
Consols & United Mines - Wheal Kitty & Blue Hills -
Tywarnhayle & Wheal Ellen

144 pages including maps, diagrams
& 60 photographs, old and new.
Glossary of mining & engineering terms.

A VIEW FROM
CARN BREA
by Bob Acton £2.95
12 round walks in the fascinating, attractive and little-known area just inland of the Helford.

LANDFALL
PUBLICATIONS
Landfall, Penpol,
Devoran, Truro, Cornwall
Tel. 01872-862581